Not Congruent but Quite Complementary

U.S. and Chinese Approaches to Nontraditional Security

Lyle J. Goldstein, Editor

CHINA MARITIME STUDIES INSTITUTE
U.S. NAVAL WAR COLLEGE
Newport, Rhode Island

www.usnwc.edu/Research---Gaming/China-Maritime-Studies-Institute.aspx

Naval War College
Newport, Rhode Island
Center for Naval Warfare Studies
China Maritime Study No. 9
July 2012

President, Naval War College
Rear Admiral John N. Christenson, U.S. Navy

Provost
Amb. Mary Ann Peters

Dean of Naval Warfare Studies
Robert C. Rubel

Director of China Maritime Studies Institute
Peter Dutton

Naval War College Press
Director: Dr. Carnes Lord
Managing Editor: Pelham G. Boyer

Telephone: 401.841.2236
Fax: 401.841.3579
DSN exchange: 841
E-mail: press@usnwc.edu
Web: www.usnwc.edu/press
www.twitter.com/NavalWarCollege

Printed in the United States of America

The China Maritime Studies are extended research projects that the editor, the Dean of Naval Warfare Studies, and the President of the Naval War College consider of particular interest to policy makers, scholars, and analysts.

Correspondence concerning the China Maritime Studies may be addressed to the director of the China Maritime Studies Institute, www.usnwc.edu/Research---Gaming/China-Maritime-Studies-Institute.aspx. To request additional copies or subscription consideration, please direct inquiries to the President, Code 32A, Naval War College, 686 Cushing Road, Newport, Rhode Island 02841-1207, or contact the Press staff at the telephone, fax, or e-mail addresses given.

Reproduction and printing is subject to the Copyright Act of 1976 and applicable treaties of the United States. This document may be freely reproduced for academic or other noncommercial use; however, it is requested that reproductions credit the author and China Maritime Studies series and that the Press editorial office be informed. To obtain permission to reproduce this publication for commercial purposes, contact the Press editorial office.

ISSN 1943-0817

ISBN 978-1-935352-04-4

Contents

Introduction, *by Lyle J. Goldstein* 1

CHAPTER ONE	The Role of NTS Issues in the China-U.S. Relationship ....5 *by Yu Wanli and Xiao He*	
CHAPTER TWO	New Directions in Chinese Security Policy .... 17 *by Bates Gill*	
CHAPTER THREE	The PLA Navy's Gulf of Aden Mission as Capability Building against NTS Threats .... 27 *by You Ji*	
CHAPTER FOUR	The PLA (Re-)Discovers Nontraditional Security .... 41 *by Andrew Scobell and Gregory Stevenson*	
CHAPTER FIVE	Issues in the Transformation of China's Engagement with International Peacekeeping .... 51 *by Pang Zhongying*	
CHAPTER SIX	Chinese Peacekeeping in the Asia Pacific: A Case Study of East Timor .... 65 *by Lyle J. Goldstein and Kathleen A. Walsh*	
CHAPTER SEVEN	Lessons from Mumbai: Chinese Analysts Assess the Threat of Maritime Terrorism .... 77 *by Sun Kai and Guo Peiqing*	
CHAPTER EIGHT	U.S. and Chinese Approaches to Peacekeeping and Stability Operations .... 87 *by Dennis J. Blasko*	
CHAPTER NINE	On China-U.S. Relations and NTS Cooperation .... 103 *by Maj. Gen. Pan Zhenqiang, People's Liberation Army (Ret.)*	
CHAPTER TEN	China's Maritime Reemergence and U.S.-China Naval Cooperation in the NTS Domain .... 117 *by Kristen Gunness*	

Abbreviations and Definitions 130
About the Contributors 133

The opinions expressed in this publication are the perspectives of the authors and do not necessarily represent the views of the U.S. Department of Defense or any of its components or the views of the government of the People's Republic of China or any of its components.

All photographs obtained with permission from China Defense Forum.

Introduction

Lyle J. Goldstein

U.S.-China relations, difficult in the best of times, have lurched in a dangerous direction since 2009. Against the backdrop of a weakened global economy and sharpened ideological tensions, there has been a disturbing new atmosphere of crisis in East Asia over the last two years, with incidents occurring in greater frequency and sowing serious doubts about the sustainability of the "long peace" that this region has enjoyed for decades. Indeed, any one of the following incidents could have escalated into a serious regional crisis: the sinking of the South Korean frigate *Cheonan*; the collision between a Japanese coast guard cutter and a Chinese fishing trawler and the ensuing Chinese restrictions on the export of rare-earth minerals; and a string of confrontations between Chinese patrol ships and vessels from both Vietnam and the Philippines.

Taken together, these incidents starkly illustrate the fundamental fragility of international security arrangements in the Asia-Pacific region and the troubling failure of the United States and China to adequately manage vexing regional challenges. In the United States and elsewhere in the West, the pervasive view is that Beijing is "feeling its oats"—eager to reap the strategic benefits of its dynamic economy even as Washington confronts major difficulties at home and abroad. Not surprisingly, Chinese observers are inclined to view these tensions differently. Difficulties with many neighboring states, such as Vietnam, are seen as encouraged and abetted by Washington, which is viewed as all too eager to exploit regional differences as a way to "contain" China's rise. Without significant course corrections in both capitals, the United States and China seem destined to follow the path of intensified rivalry that may even lead to the possibility of large-scale armed conflict. As Henry Kissinger has recently written, this path is "the road to disaster."[1]

Facing such difficult circumstances, some observers in the United States are inclined to exert new and extraordinary efforts for the purposes of enhancing military deterrence. Aaron Friedberg, for example, argues that the "U.S. position in Asia must appear so strong and so resilient that Beijing will ultimately choose to stand down rather than risk everything."[2] By contrast, this assembled volume describes a much more hopeful and cooperative approach. Surveying global security over the last two decades, the collection makes it apparent that both sides of the Pacific frequently articulate surprisingly similar security concerns—such as terrorism, the proliferation of weapons of mass destruction, piracy, environmental crisis, humanitarian disaster, ethnic strife, and economic dislocation—all of which are issues that sit under the "large tent" of nontraditional security (NTS) concerns. To be sure, traditional security threats remain a regional concern. But scholars, practitioners, and leaders in international security—including recently retired secretary of defense Robert Gates—are all focusing new energy on issues that are decidedly different from classic strategies of interstate conflict and zero-sum outcomes.[3] Unfortunately, relatively few academic studies have fully explored the potential for overlap in American and Chinese interests with respect to NTS.

An especially noteworthy contribution to the field of international relations and one that takes the U.S.-China cooperation problem with due seriousness is Michael Swaine's recent *America's Challenge: Engaging a Rising China in the Twenty-First Century*. According to Swaine, "America's strategy toward China will need to place a much greater emphasis on cooperation instead of rivalry."[4] Moreover, Swaine argues not only that NTS cooperation between the United States and China could build the trust necessary to tackle more challenging problems but also that "without strong U.S.-China cooperation, such transnational threats will prove virtually impossible to manage."[5] Thus, successful U.S.-China cooperation is not simply imperative for Asia-Pacific security but will also be key to global governance more generally.

The present volume reflects a commitment to develop international maritime cooperation between the United States and China through academic dialogue—and also to the careful examination of unique Chinese perspectives on critical issues related to NTS. It is the result of the China Maritime Studies Institute's annual conference in Newport during May 2010, which involved the participation of almost a dozen Chinese specialist presenters, who were able to exchange ideas with their American counterparts. It is worth noting that despite a major effort to invite wide PLA Navy participation in this conference, the Chinese navy ultimately declined to attend, because of political difficulties in the bilateral relationship. Despite this initial setback, the conference was quite successful, as the insightful chapters that follow will demonstrate. For their help in planning the initial conference, I wish to acknowledge the major assistance of Mr. Dalton Alexander and Lt. Cdr. Edward Fiorentino, as well as Naval War College faculty members Professor Andrew Erickson and Professor Kathleen Walsh.

The volume is unique in several respects, and not only because it offers both Chinese and American perspectives side by side. First and foremost, the assembled papers offer a glimpse into the rapidly developing and wide-ranging Chinese-language discussion about NTS issues and their role in Beijing's future foreign policy. A plethora of Chinese citations attest to the careful efforts that have been made to synthesize this important literature, heretofore largely inaccessible to Western scholars. In addition, the volume includes both the views of policy insiders and also the ideas of individuals outside of government. Indeed, many of the authors do not shy away from challenging current policies. What this volume is *not* is a rote recitation of "happy talk." The analyses are clear-eyed about certain limits with respect to NTS capabilities and sensitive regarding the implications of certain divergent views on NTS issues for the bilateral relationship overall. The assembled papers broadly assess the full scope of the bilateral NTS relationship and simultaneously dive deeply into crucial case studies, in such vital areas as counterpiracy and peacekeeping. Finally, as befits the work of an institute focused on maritime studies, there is a distinct focus on maritime issues, including a chapter on maritime counterterrorism, without ignoring key developments ashore that are crucial components to addressing any NTS challenges and to furthering the bilateral relationship as a whole.

A strong consensus at the conference and among the chapters that follow emerges that new Chinese interest in and capabilities for NTS operations offer a vital strategic opportunity to enhance U.S.-China security cooperation. The chapters also reveal that while American and Chinese viewpoints on NTS issues are hardly congruent, they are surprisingly complementary. It is therefore hoped that this volume will help to build the foundation of a more cooperative pursuit of Chinese and American national interests and of international security more generally.

Notes

1. Henry Kissinger, *On China* (New York: Penguin Press, 2011), p. 528.
2. Aaron L. Friedberg, *A Contest for Supremacy: America, China and the Struggle for Mastery in Asia* (New York: W. W. Norton, 2011), p. 275.
3. See, for example, Julian B. Earnes, "Win Today's War, Gates Says," *Los Angeles Times,* 14 May 2008.
4. Michael D. Swaine, *America's Challenge: Engaging a Rising China in the Twenty-First Century* (Washington, D.C.: Carnegie, 2011), p. 18.
5. Ibid., p. 7.

The Role of NTS Issues in the China-U.S. Relationship

Yu Wanli and Xiao He

In China, many new changes in the minds of leaders and also within society have finally made the nontraditional security (NTS) concept acceptable, even as Chinese features are inevitably etched in it. Today the NTS concept amounts in China to much more than academic terminology but also forms a genuine policy guideline, one that directly affects China's foreign policy. Although the NTS concept in China represents the state's special attention to comprehensive strategy, its development is also clearly the result of China's learning from the outside world since 1978. Initially, such learning was involuntary, nonstrategic, and reactive. During the decade and a half since the adoption of NTS concepts, development of the concept was pursued mainly as a means to achieve other goals, one of which was to reduce U.S. political pressure and to render futile American hostility. After the 9/11 terrorist attacks, however, the situation changed abruptly. Thereafter, American pressure was much reduced, the strategic space for China grew swiftly, and China's attitude toward the concept of NTS finally shifted in favor of volunteering to participate in NTS efforts as a key dimension of a systematic strategy. China may have learned about NTS from European or other regions, but Washington's disposition—either friendly or hostile—was consistently the primary factor in the development of China's strategy. The U.S. factor continues today to be an extremely important variable in any examination of China's approach to NTS.

China's Approach to NTS

As early as 1989, China first employed environmental diplomacy by hosting a multinational conference to discuss environmental protection through global cooperation, even though there was no genuine domestic requirement to pursue that issue. Beijing saw that conference as a breakthrough in the political "blockade line" of the United States and saw it as a good model for other potential activities. This episode reveals the reactive nature of the very origin of China's approach to NTS issues. In most cases, China could do no more than make declarations, rather than propose constructive plans, because it lacked the requisite specialized knowledge.

A subsequent stage, the eight years from 1992 to 2000, was the foreshadowing of today's NTS, in that the phrase "new security view" came into being in official literature. During this period Chinese policy makers felt an acute threat from the United States, based on such crises as the *Yinhe* incident in 1993, the naval confrontation in the Taiwan Strait in 1996, the bombing of the People's Republic of China embassy in Belgrade in 1999, and the Hainan Island incident in 2001. Facing such serious challenges from the United States, China decided to deter American hegemony by enhancing its relationships with other states. The "new security view" was first mentioned at the Association of Southeast Asian Nations (ASEAN) Regional Forum in 1995, and then at conferences with Central Asian countries. However there was no exact definition of such new ideas until the Geneva Conference on Disarmament in 1999. During that conference, Chinese president Jiang Zemin pointed out that the core principles of the new security view were "mutual trust, mutual benefit, equality and cooperation." Moreover, he emphasized, "history tells us we can neither secure our nations nor realize worldwide perpetual peace guided by the old security view, which was based on military alliances and arm races." The new security view, therefore, focused on denying the utility of military violence and emphasized the importance of international cooperation, not transnational or substate actors.

The NTS concept was first introduced to China in 1994, but it was not until 1999 that the first academic paper concerning NTS was published.[1] In June 2001, Beijing promoted the NTS concept at the Shanghai Cooperation Organization summit, on the one hand displaying its attention to cooperation in counterterrorism, antiextremism, and antiseparatism issues, but on the other hand seeking new allies to resist growing U.S. deterrence measures. To some extent, before the September 2001 attacks the new security view and NTS were both aimed at encouraging any process that would restrain U.S. power.[2]

But the September 11th terrorist attack changed the whole situation. Beijing entered a third stage of thinking about the role of NTS, as it realized that NTS cooperation with Washington not only was possible, but also could be extremely beneficial to China. After the attacks, China quickly decided to grasp the opportunity to enhance its relationship with the George W. Bush administration. In October, China agreed to add antiterrorism issues to the agenda of the Asia-Pacific Economic Cooperation (APEC) meetings and published a declaration in support of Bush's actions against terrorism. China then cast an affirmative vote on United Nations (UN) Security Council Resolution 1368, which gave legitimacy to U.S. military actions in Afghanistan. These policies were clear departures from China's previous stances, and China soon reaped the reward for its cooperation. In August 2002, the United States officially listed the East Turkestan Islamic Movement as a terrorist organization.

Beginning at that time, the concept of NTS appeared with increasing frequency in China's formal, official statements. At the ASEAN Regional Forum in July 2002, for instance, China stressed the importance of NTS in its *Position Paper of China's New Security View*. Then, in November, the Sixteenth Party Congress Report of the Chinese

Communist Party (CCP) stated that "traditional security and nontraditional security are intertwined," and in December, *China's National Defense 2002* mentioned NTS, even asserting that nontraditional security was an important task for national defense.

Simultaneously, the content of NTS concepts expanded. In 2003, the severe acute respiratory syndrome (SARS) epidemic constituted a warning to all Chinese concerning the vulnerability of China's public sanitary system. In that year, China and ASEAN held a special summit to discuss prevention of an epidemic, and through newspaper and television reports on the summit the term "nontraditional security" became familiar not only to Chinese leaders but also to ordinary Chinese citizens. Chinese people began increasingly to discuss many new aspects of "security," such as social security, energy security, food security, environmental security, and financial security. In the *Chinese Government White Book: China's Path of Peaceful Development (2005–2006),* Chinese leaders connected reduction of terrorism, financial risk, and natural disasters to the maintenance of world peace, security, and stability through cooperation. Now the concept of NTS is trendy, to be sure, but nevertheless also genuinely urgent.

Definitions and Chinese Tendencies

NTS issues originate primarily from within a state's social structures rather than through another state's hostile intention or actions. NTS issues, moreover, do not threaten national sovereignty or integrity; rather, they create victims among ordinary citizens or groups in society. When the NTS problems expand to other countries, they primarily endanger foreign individuals and groups.

From the very beginning, China's government accepted this concept selectively and revised it according to its own thinking. Though the Chinese government embraces NTS sincerely, its leaders never try to abase the position of the state, either practically or theoretically. Beijing is always extremely uncomfortable when it finds itself alongside nonstate actors, especially nongovernmental organizations (NGOs). On the one hand, Chinese leaders admit that NTS issues are so complex that they require international cooperation. On the other hand, Beijing has the confidence to handle domestic NTS issues on its own. This approach is explained, of course, by the fact that China is highly sensitive on issues related to its sovereign authority. The Chinese government tries its best to put all kinds of social forces into official tracks. For instance, the government required that all donations for rebuilding the town of Yushu after a serious earthquake be distributed by one, semiofficial organization. All other, direct methods of donation were forbidden. For the same reason, China will not accept a hard international verification system on any issue, such as reduction of carbon emissions. In addition to these most important characteristics, China's perspectives on NTS are constructed on two tracks, step by step, in both the domestic and international contexts, and especially within the context of China-U.S. relations.

Securitization in China

In *Security: A New Framework for Analysis,* Barry Buzan, Ole Wæver, and Jaap de Wilde describe an interesting concept—"securitization."[3] Securitization is the process through which public issues become security issues that require the special attention of the state. Securitized issues must always be handled and resourced by the government. Therefore, securitization is politicization, since security represents the highest interest of politics. However, there is no objective standard to judge what is actually a security issue and what is nothing more than a social construct of the whole society.

Since 2002, when the Chinese government began to use NTS terminology, every industry and department of the government has wanted to connect itself with this security issue. At first this process was relatively slow and focused on issues of national scope. In 2003, for instance, China became a net importer of petroleum, and thereafter concerns were frequently voiced about "energy security." The concept expanded in 2004, when China imported eight million tons of wheat to satisfy its domestic requirements. This stimulated the Chinese government to emphasize the importance of "food security." The Chinese food company Wahaha accused the French competitor Danone of endangering Chinese "economic security" and called for industrial protection—prompting some Chinese newspapers to react with sarcasm ("We find cookies and beverages have become national security issues this morning") and despite the facts that China's self-sufficiency rate of grain is always nearly 95 percent (much higher than the approximately 40 percent in Japan) and in 2007 the Chinese government approved a policy to create biofuels from food crops.[4]

At the same time, the concept of the "Malacca Dilemma" (in reference to the criticality and apparent vulnerability of the Straits of Malacca for Chinese imports) became pervasive in the Chinese press, a dilemma backed by two pillars—gigantic, state-owned oil companies and the PLA Navy. On one side, oil companies warned the central government to grasp a more stable foreign crude-oil supply and build more continental pipelines. On the other side, the PLA Navy advocated construction of fleets to protect energy lanes, including the Malacca Strait. These two players, along with the hard-line press, successfully established the "Malacca Dilemma" concept in the minds of Chinese society, hiding the facts that the price of oil in international futures markets can never recover the real costs of such pipeline projects and that future Chinese fleets would not be capable of protecting ships transporting oil to China.

Ironically, it is China's "public security" apparatus that has been most fully tested by these tendencies toward securitization. Educated by the SARS crisis and other related incidents, the Chinese people are increasingly willing to struggle for their own rights and interests in the name of "securities." In the next decade or two, China will likely enter a period of frequent social conflict.[5] Building a system that can maintain social stability and security is a vitally important goal for China, because the NTS problems inside China are just as serious as those external to China.

China-U.S. Interaction in NTS Issues

Washington prefers to talk about single-issue areas rather than to employ the umbrella term "nontraditional security," in part because the NTS concept was born with a certain anti-U.S. complexion. As mentioned above, China, conversely, was glad to use the NTS concept and emphasize its growing importance, in quiet reproach to Washington. But even if the United States is uncomfortable with the terminology, it must agree that nontraditional security issues have contributed quite a lot to the China-U.S. relationship. From China's viewpoint, there are three main characteristics of interaction with the United States in the domain of NTS issues.

First, the Chinese people and government have the impression that trade is one of Washington's most important national goals. For instance, beginning in the late 1990s the U.S. Department of State made China an important target for cooperation in environmental diplomacy. This cooperation was focused on encouraging China's Environment Ministry to purchase American equipment and technology in large amounts. Whether or not the U.S. government relaxes its trade restrictions on high-end technologies continues to be a good litmus test of Washington's true attitude toward China.

Second, in China's official public statements the politicization of trade and monetary negotiations between China and the United States is unfortunately portrayed as the main threat to China's economic security. The endless discussion and debate in the United States concerning whether to label China a currency manipulator strains China's patience and angers its citizens. Due to the transparency of various U.S. legal procedures, ordinary Chinese people get a relatively clear picture of America's intentions and methods, some of which are inevitably harmful to China's interests. Therefore, conspiracy theories about the U.S. government usually prevail in China.

Third, the United States has altered its method of persuading China to accept and maintain the present international order. In the past, the primary method was to convince China to be a "responsible stakeholder," as Robert Zoellick put it. After 2001, even by American standards China was taking more and more responsibility, had changed its attitude toward international nonproliferation, and had adopted export-control regulations on missile, biological, and chemical materials. Still, in 2005 Zoellick warned that China could not achieve energy security by pursuing oil deals with countries that the United States considered troublesome and indicated that the approach would only result in conflict with the United States.[6]

Now, in addition to continuing to encourage China to be responsible, the United States has begun to accept China's unique interests. Although Deputy Secretary of State James B. Steinberg's fall 2009 speech on "strategic reassurance" still reminds China to "reassure the rest of the world that its development and growing global role will not come at the expense of the security and well-being of others,"[7] it also provides a clear promise to support China's development. In a word, Washington is trying to publicize China's successes in following American counsel. It seems as though Washington will finally accommodate China's interests in the long-term and to some degree share resources and leadership with China. Thus, China has obtained oil business in the Gulf of Mexico and Iraq and copper interests in Afghanistan, reflecting that the United States has begun to treat China as a responsible leader, not just a responsible player. It is evident that cooperation on NTS issues has at various times improved the China-U.S. relationship.

Respective Priorities

Secretary of State Hillary Rodham Clinton and Deputy Secretary Steinberg have articulated U.S. NTS priorities.[8] First, confronting the global economic crisis is the core challenge of the Barack Obama administration, and accordingly the Sino-American trade imbalance and related currency issues remain a point of bilateral contention. A second major priority, of equal importance to the economic issues, is the goal of strengthening the global nonproliferation regime. Washington requires Beijing's support in the UN to block Iran's and North Korea's nuclear ambitions. Third, the Obama administration is advancing technologies and promoting cooperation to mitigate climate change, especially after the Copenhagen Conference, in which China and the United States gained mutual understanding but failed to reach any specific accords.

In addition to these three goals, in the past few years the U.S. government has increasingly emphasized the importance of the "global commons"—including the seas, air, space, and cyberspace. For instance, the United States has led regional cooperative efforts to counter piracy in Southeast Asia and views them as a success case. Now it also encourages many countries, including China, to protect East Africa's international sea-lanes. Recently, the United States has viewed China's behavior in the South China Sea as reflecting a preference toward exclusive access and hence has reacted swiftly. This has caused several new contradictions between Beijing and Washington. The openness of the global commons is seen by some in the United States as the organizing principle by which to cope with all NTS issues and thus indispensable to U.S. national interests.

From Beijing's perspective, the most important NTS issue is undoubtedly economic security, which is endangered not only by the global financial crisis but also by the significant pressure exerted on China by the U.S. government, and especially Congress. Moreover, economic growth in China has recently encountered two serious challenges. The first is, as the latest financial crisis illustrates, that the Chinese economy is too dependent on exports. Just as the U.S. government says, China needs to complete its economic restructuring and develop its domestic market, which should be large and dynamic enough to sustain long-term economic growth. The second issue is that when an economy grows, the cost of such growth increases ever more quickly. Such costs are closely tied to three critical NTS issues in China.

First is the problem of maintaining China's "overriding stability," which consumes more and more resources, since any single social problem may cause a crisis of confidence in the Chinese government and even result in massive and violent upheaval. Budget reports demonstrate that in 2009 China's financial expenditure on public security increased 47.5 percent over 2008, to 128.7 billion yuan.[9] Second, as wealth and industrial capacity grow, the need for energy and other key inputs increases, even as China can no longer satisfy this demand by itself or through various oil pipelines. Therefore, China has been required to cooperate with many remote countries to ensure its energy security, including countries as unpopular with America as Sudan and Iran. Also, the fact that China's import of energy and raw materials is dependent on maritime transport makes sea-lane security a new core interest of China. This significant development largely explains the efforts of China's fleet off Somalia's coast. Third, it may be said that the threat of global warming is less urgent to China but that the low efficiency, high energy consumption, and high pollution rate of China's industries are certainly of urgent concern. China shows great interest in cooperation on clean energy and other technologies that can improve efficiency while decreasing energy consumption and pollution. China's attitude toward carbon emission reduction is sincere, although it believes that such attempts should decrease and not increase the cost of China's continuing economic development.

To be sure, American and Chinese priorities with respect to NTS issues are not exactly congruent. But just as former ambassador Jon Huntsman said, "our leaders recognize this, which is why they concentrated on getting to know one another better and defining our priorities together."[10] This suggests that neither China nor America can pursue its own goals by damaging the other's interest in NTS issues, because of the "balance of financial terror" that exists between the two countries. It also suggests that through cooperation both can achieve much more than they can through independent actions. Perhaps China and the United States cannot reach a consensus, now or in the foreseeable future, on such issues as weapons sales to Taiwan or meetings with the Dalai Lama, but the imperative for wider cooperation is becoming nonetheless ever more obvious.

Huntsman routinely repeated during his tenure as ambassador that "we have to delink our differences on the bilateral track from our cooperation on the global track." This statement seems both realistic and reasonable.

Prospects for China-U.S. NTS Cooperation

Although suspicion and anger continue in the South China Sea between Beijing and Washington, maritime strategy, which is closely related to several key NTS issues, remains one of the most promising realms for China-U.S. cooperation. This cooperation is very important, because there is no sound military-to-military communication system, even as contacts between units of the U.S. and Chinese navies are becoming increasingly frequent. The consequence of that situation is that more and more maritime contradictions arise in the maritime domain and hostility between the two navies grows. During the Obama administration alone, several serious incidents have occurred, including the USNS *Impeccable* incident and U.S. naval exercises in the Yellow Sea. The main cause of such crises is that mutual understanding regarding naval strategy is simply inadequate.

China's stance is that its development of asymmetric naval power, such as advanced antiship cruise missiles and submarines, is totally defensive and focused on preventing Taiwan's possible separation. Chinese navy commanders have a clear understanding that the Chinese navy is much weaker than that of the United States. Therefore, American requests to Chinese leaders for more transparency seem rather hostile. Chinese military leaders believe the United States has no need to worry about the Chinese navy unless the United States wants to invade the Chinese coastline or limit Chinese naval power.

It is perplexing that the defensive weapons of the Chinese navy are portrayed as more dangerous than the aircraft carriers of the U.S. Navy. The development of anti-intervention weapons by China has been termed an "antiaccess" capability by the United States, which suggests that China prefers to create areas that exclude access by the United States. The expedition of the Chinese flotilla to the Gulf of Aden has not stimulated the "China threat" theory but has received wide affirmation and praise, but the Chinese declaration that included the South China Sea issue among China's core interests resulted in rapid diplomatic countermeasures by Washington.

Overall, in naval strategy China has always underestimated the determination of the United States to protect the global commons and its "free for all" principle, while the United States has failed to persuade China to accept its view toward the seas or to dismantle China's underlying suspicions regarding the sincerity of Washington's positive attitude toward a powerful Chinese navy. To overcome this mutual suspicion requires cooperation in both traditional and nontraditional security issues, and the latter looks more easy and realistic, as Beijing focuses on the bilateral track and Washington focuses more on the global track.

The Center for a New American Security (CNAS) has described the four broad characteristics of the global commons, which are of vital importance to the U.S. comprehensive civil and military capabilities:

- They are not owned or controlled by any single entity.
- Their utility as a whole is greater than if broken down into smaller parts.
- States and nonstate actors with the requisite technological capabilities are able to access and use them for economic, political, scientific, and cultural purposes.
- States and nonstate actors with the requisite technological capabilities are able to use them as a medium for military movement and as a theater for military conflict.[11]

This rendering of the global commons makes them useful and important not only for the United States but also for China. However, the United States can benefit much more than China from the global commons—the seas, space, or cyberspace. Therefore, to convince China, the United States first needs to encourage the improvement of China's capabilities—especially its blue-water navy, which does not pose a threat to the U.S. Navy. Such encouragement will demonstrate America's sincerity to the Chinese government and ordinary people, and a more powerful navy will likely cause China to reconsider the values of a "free use" principle, similar to the process by which China turned to the "free trade" principle.

Acts of Piracy by Region and Year
Source: International Maritime Organization. Year to date, Jan. 1–Sept. 30, 2009.

Region	2003	2004	2005	2006	2007	2008	2009
Far East	4	11	10	2	3	0	18
Southeast Asia	185	162	112	86	77	62	32
South Asia	87	32	37	53	30	23	22
Middle East	3	5	12	7	11	?	15
East Africa	29	15	53	29	66	42	153
West Africa	64	58	27	32	54	61	32
Latin America	71	44	25	29	21	17	28
Other	2	2	0	1	1	1	6
Total	445	329	276	239	263	206 +	306

Second, the United States should encourage China to increase its participation with respect to maritime NTS issues, such as the antipiracy mission. As the table indicates, although piracy has decreased in certain areas, such as Southeast Asia, since 2008, overall acts of piracy have flourished. There still remains an imperative to get China

The Chinese navy has embraced the concept of nontraditional security. In particular, the continuing Chinese counterpiracy operations in the Gulf of Aden have given the PLA Navy much needed blue-water experience, including practice with boardings, as illustrated here.

more involved in this issue, and this participation will encourage China's naval force to become ever more transparent. On this point, the United States has praised the actions of Chinese squadrons in the waters off Somalia several times and in different cases. Washington should continue this policy and, to some degree, share leadership on this issue with China rather than deliberately damaging China's prestige by provoking conflicts between China and its maritime neighbors.

Another promising issue is cooperation to achieve energy security, which has gone positively between China and the United States in recent years. As James Steinberg notes, "When the President visited Beijing last November, we had adopted a package of measures including a new clean energy research center, an electrical vehicles initiative, and a renewable energy partnership."[12] As Steinberg's summary shows, cooperation on energy issues should be based on two pillars. The first is on the transfer of technology, which can bring revenue to the United States; the second concerns the construction of a new energy-distribution network based on the mutual recognition of the other's interests.

Though plans to build various oil pipelines have never been abandoned by China and some of them have indeed been realized, China still cannot overcome the influence of both Russia and the United States to achieve more complete access to Caspian Sea energy resources. China's somewhat zero-sum, unilateral approach to enhancing its oil security not only fuels American wariness regarding China's strengthening ties with oil-producing countries like Iran and Sudan but damages the prestige of the Chinese government in some cases, as in the Darfur crisis. China needs to decrease the risks and costs of its attempts to enhance its energy security.

Washington seems to recognize that only sharing oil resources with China can provide a stable basis for Sino-American strategic cooperation. Shared business with Saudi Arabia, which is the most important U.S. ally in the Persian Gulf region, and also with Mexico and Iraq, is a good model. If this trend can be sustained, cooperation on the energy issue will significantly strengthen the Sino-American relationship. This is especially true since the issue of the "balance of financial terror" must be confronted by both states. Perhaps on this firm foundation, trust between these two countries can finally be established, further enabling constructive cooperation on traditional security issues.

The Revival of Traditional Security

In the first term of Obama's presidency there have been periods of tension and of ease in the China-U.S. relationship. Periods of tensions are always driven by traditional security issues, such as the territorial disputes along China's maritime periphery. Fortunately, however, these tensions are not the main current. The trend toward cooperation in the bilateral relationship remains the norm, and many observers see this kind of swing between tension and cooperation as in itself normal.

The Chinese government is quite willing to take responsibility in international affairs and to improve relations with other countries concerning NTS. But this requires Beijing to take some risk. For instance, after the serious earthquake and the tsunami in Japan, China's significant overtures received a rather cold reception in Japan; this initiative to cooperate was not necessarily viewed as a success. Nevertheless, both China and America need to deepen and enlarge their cooperation on NTS issues. The death of Bin Laden was seen as definite good news in China, more sincerely than it would have been years before, as terrorist incidents in Xinjiang occur more frequently. Still, there can be further cooperation on counterterrorism issues.

Moreover, the recent accident involving a Chinese high-speed train reminds the Chinese people that the gap between developed states and China is still wide and that there remain many things to learn. A more powerful China will need the United States even more. For instance, when China dispatched the missile frigate *Xuzhou* to Libya to rescue its citizens in danger, it became clear that future such rescue missions will require the help, tutelage, and cooperation of the U.S. Navy. Now that the Chinese navy is equipped with an aircraft carrier, there are new opportunities to advance NTS cooperation beyond the economic issues.

Notes

1. 余潇枫, 李佳 [Yu Xiaofeng and Li Jia], "非传统安全：中国的认知与应对(1978～2008)年" [Nontraditional Security: China's Acknowledgement and Response (1978–2008)], 世界经济与政治 [World Economy and Politics], no. 11 (2008).
2. Lee Pak and Chan Lai-Ha, "Non-Traditional Security Threat in China: Challenges of Energy Shortage and Infectious Disease" in *Challenges and Policy Programmes of China's New Leadership*, ed. Joseph Cheng (Hong Kong: City Univ. of Hong Kong Press, 2007), pp. 297–336.
3. Barry Buzan, Ole Wæver, and Jaap de Wilde, *Security: A New Framework for Analysis* (Boulder, Colo.: Lynne Rienner, 1998).
4. 刘宇, 查道炯 [Liu Yu and Zha Daojiong], "粮食问题的中国认知 (1979–2009)" [China's Acknowledgement of Food Issues (1979–2009)], 国际政治研究 [International Politics Research], no. 2 (2010).
5. Yu Jianrong, "Social Conflicts in China," *China Security* 3, no. 2 (Spring 2007).
6. Robert Zoellick, "Whither China: From Membership to Responsibility" (speech to the National Committee on U.S.-China Relations, 21 September 2005), available at www.ncuscr.org/files/2005Gala_RobertZoellick_Whither_China1.pdf
7. James B. Steinberg, "Keynote Address" (remarks, Center for New American Security, Washington, D.C., 5 October 2009), available at www.cnas.org/node/3466.
8. James B. Steinberg, *Rising Powers and Global Institutions: World Order in the 21st Century* (remarks at the Council on Foreign Relations, Washington, D.C., 19 May 2010).
9. *People's Daily,* 5 March 2010.
10. Jon Huntsman, "2010: The Year of Decision" (remarks of the U.S. ambassador to the People's Republic of China, Tsinghua Univ., Beijing, 18 March 2010), available at beijing.usembassy-china.org.cn/031810amb.html.
11. Abraham M. Denmark and Dr. James Mulvenon, eds., *Contested Commons: The Future of American Power in a Multipolar World* (Washington, D.C.: Center for a New American Security, January 2010).
12. James B. Steinberg (Deputy Secretary of State), *U.S.-China Cooperation on Global Issues* (Washington, D.C.: Brookings Institution, 11 May 2010).

New Directions in Chinese Security Policy

Bates Gill

The growth of China's role on the global stage, while in process for nearly two decades, seems to have accelerated in recent years. The global financial crisis of 2008–2009 had the effect of promoting even more China's global position as a country able to avoid the worst of the crisis and appear as a relatively stable economic and financial partner for the world. China's high-profile participation in the G-20 summits in Washington (2008) and in London and Pittsburgh (2009) were a kind of "coming out" party for Beijing and its augmented global role. President Barack Obama's state visit to China in November 2009 resulted in a remarkably wide-ranging and detailed joint statement, covering the full sweep of U.S.-China relations.[1] But in 2010 and 2011, many observers in the West and in East Asia sensed that China was beginning to throw its newfound weight around too much, overreaching and asserting its interests in unhelpful ways around its periphery—such as in the South China Sea—and around the globe. This is all the more reason for analysts to take stock of China's growing role and the evolution of China's security policy that undergirds it. Is it justifiable to say that today is a period of "new directions" for Chinese security policy? If so, what are the drivers that shape these new directions, and how are these new directions manifested? What are some of the interesting research and policy implications posed by such new directions?

A Look Back at the Evolution of China's New Foreign and Security Policy

Since the mid-1990s, China has taken up positions on regional and global security matters that are more consistent with broad international norms and practice than in the past. China's approach to regional and global security affairs has become increasingly proactive, practical, and constructive. Through a combination of pragmatic security policies, growing economic clout, and increasingly deft diplomacy, China has established productive relationships throughout Asia and around the globe, including new partnerships in Southeast Asia, Central Asia, Europe, Africa, and South America. These developments have unfolded at a time, since the early 2000s, of strategic preoccupation on the part of the United States: prosecuting major military operations in Afghanistan and Iraq, conducting a global counterterrorism campaign, and digging out of the financial meltdown and economic recession of 2008–2009. American preoccupation, in turn, has opened even greater strategic space for China to expand its influence within the region and indeed at global levels.

This "new direction" in Chinese foreign and security policy is well established and traces its roots to the early 1980s and the strategic verdict reached at the time by Deng Xiaoping—that the world was tending toward peace and development, the possibility of a world war was remote, and China could expect a stable international environment in which it could carry out much-needed domestic development. Despite many shifts in the international environment since that time, the basic Chinese approach to foreign and security policy has rested on the same assumption, that the overall tendency of world affairs is toward peace and development, increased multipolarity and economic globalization, and a general easing of tensions.

By the late 1990s and early 2000s, while not explicitly stated as such, China's strategic assumptions and principles began to gel more distinctly into recognizable goals. These fundamental goals provided the underlying motivations for China's new security diplomacy. First, the Chinese leadership generally sought to maintain a stable international environment in order to defuse instabilities, especially around its periphery, so Beijing could focus on critical economic, political, and social challenges at home. Second, China's new security diplomacy obviously aimed to augment China's wealth and influence, but in a way that tried to reassure its neighbors of its peaceful and mutually beneficial intent. Beijing had come to understand the security-dilemma dynamic and wished to avoid alarming its neighbors; instead, it promoted the notion of a "harmonious world." Third, the new security diplomacy sought to counter, co-opt, or circumvent what Beijing perceived as excessive American influence around the Chinese periphery while avoiding overt confrontation with the United States, all with the aim of shaping its security environment in ways consistent with Chinese interests.

Consistent with these three goals, Beijing's new approach was readily apparent in its more constructive policies across a range of security issues, including such activities as participating in regional security mechanisms and confidence-building measures, improving its nonproliferation and arms-control policies at home and abroad, expanding its peacekeeping and counterterrorism activities, taking a slightly more flexible approach to issues of sovereignty and intervention, and showing some greater willingness to shoulder more responsibilities as an emerging great power. According to *Liaowang (Outlook),* the Chinese Communist Party weekly general-affairs journal,

> Compared with past practices, China's diplomacy has indeed displayed a new face. If China's diplomacy before the 1980s stressed safeguarding of national security and its emphasis from the 1980s to early this century was on the creation of an excellent environment for economic development, then the focus at present is to take a more active part in

international affairs and play a role that a responsible power should on the basis of satisfying the security and development interests.[2]

Beijing's New Assertiveness?

Compared to its past diplomacy, China's foreign and security policy since the mid-1990s has demonstrated a remarkable shift in direction across a host of important issues. The question going forward is whether this trend will continue, slow, or possibly reverse, or whether even more dramatic "new directions" are in store. Over the course of 2010 and 2011, for example, many observers noted that China pursued a more "assertive" and "abrasive" posture both at home and abroad. But these policies, while worrisome, probably do not signal a major new shift in direction for China, at least for the near to medium term.

Rather, the fundamental factors motivating China's generally more constructive foreign and security policy remain in place. First, China's security diplomacy is still largely shaped by a need to maintain stable and productive external relations in order to ensure socioeconomic development at home. Second, China's security diplomacy still aims to reassure its neighbors of the country's peaceful intentions as Beijing recognizes the need to maintain stable relations around its periphery in order, again, to foster continued development at home. Third, Chinese security diplomacy still seeks to counter but not openly confront what Beijing sees as excessive American influence around the Chinese periphery.

China's domestic economic, social, and political development challenges have intensified in many respects in recent years precisely as a result of ongoing economic growth and heightened social and political expectations within parts of the Chinese population. The income gap in China between rich and poor continues to expand, greater and greater development pressures are building on Chinese resources, and the need to import foreign capital, goods, and technologies continues to grow. Increased social and economic development has apparently not quelled resentment among some of China's less advantaged populations, including workers, farmers, and some ethnic and religious minorities, as in Tibet and Xinjiang.

Moreover, the increasing impact of "nontraditional" security concerns on Chinese national interests also suggests that Beijing will continue its generally more practical and constructive security diplomacy.[3] Chinese leaders and strategists—traditional guardians of state sovereignty, typically reluctant to consider bilateral or multilateral steps that might lead to "meddling" in others' internal affairs—have nevertheless increasingly acknowledged that the spread of transnational security problems has blurred state borders. Moreover, there is increasingly an understanding in China that these challenges affect Chinese security. Many of the most challenging issues the Chinese leadership will face over the coming years are transnational in nature: the impact of globalization on China's domestic economy; environmental degradation, water shortages, and energy access; the spread of HIV/AIDS, avian influenza, and other infectious diseases; proliferation of nuclear technologies and materials; and what Beijing calls the three evils—terrorism, separatism, and extremism—as well as other types of transborder crime, such as drug trafficking, gunrunning, smuggling, and piracy. Dealing with these challenges to China's national interests will demand that Chinese security diplomacy continue to take a collaborative approach.

Nontraditional Security Challenges: Chinese Contributions to Peace Operations

One area of activity where China has shown far greater willingness to address nontraditional security concerns is engagement in peace and stability operations.[4] China now deploys more than twenty times as many peacekeepers to United Nations (UN) peace operations as it did in 2000. China ranks among the top fifteen countries contributing personnel to UN peace operations and since the mid-2000s has consistently provided more troops, police, and observers to them than any other permanent member of the UN Security Council. By engaging more deeply in peacekeeping and providing engineers, transport battalions, and medical units, China contributes critically needed material assets—and perceived legitimacy—at a time when multilateral peacekeeping is severely overstretched.

Chinese "blue helmets" operating in Africa. Beijing is the leading contributor of troops to United Nations peacekeeping operations among the permanent five (P-5) states in the UN Security Council.

China has also increased its engagement in other activities related to peace and stability operations. As part of an overall effort to "go out to learn," People's Liberation Army (PLA) officers have been sent to take part in professional training and exchanges on peacekeeping operations in countries including Australia, Bangladesh, Canada, Estonia, Germany, Hungary, India, Indonesia, Ireland, Italy, Mongolia, New Zealand, Norway, South Africa, Sweden, Switzerland, and Thailand. Chinese officers have also participated, either as observers or as active participants, in peacekeeping training exercises organized under the French Reinforcement of African Peacekeeping Capabilities (RECAMP) initiative, as well as those sponsored by the British defense and security establishments. The PLA has requested some foreign military counterparts to provide it additional help and more rigorous peacekeeping training programs.

China has also organized and hosted a number of international seminars on peacekeeping affairs. For example, since 2004 it has hosted the annual United Kingdom–China Seminar on Peacekeeping Operations. China has also arranged similar seminars with Norway and Sweden. The International Committee of the Red Cross has provided seminars and predeployment briefings on international humanitarian law for Chinese peacekeepers.[5] In 2007 the Chinese Office of Peacekeeping Affairs sponsored the first China–Association of Southeast Asian Nations (ASEAN) peacekeeping seminar in Beijing. More recently, at the 2009 China-ASEAN High Level Defense Dialogue, senior PLA officials reiterated the country's commitment to cooperation on peacekeeping, including training.[6]

China has also significantly increased its engagement in joint military exercises with foreign militaries in recent years, frequently focusing on nontraditional security issues. The first such exercises, referred to as "joint counterterrorism exercises," were collaborations between China and its partners in the Shanghai Cooperation Organization (SCO) in October 2002 and 2003. These were followed by similar counterterrorism exercises held with Pakistan and, shortly afterward, in August 2004, with India. In September 2006, Chinese and Tajik troops carried out a joint military exercise, named CO-ORDINATION 2006, in which they simulated a hostage-taking scenario. STRIKE 2007, a two-week joint counterterrorism training exercise involving sixty specialized Chinese and Thai troops, was held in July 2007 in China's Guangdong Province. China and Mongolia held their first joint military training exercise, PEACEKEEPING MISSION 2009, in June and July 2009. The Chinese white paper on national defense issued in March 2011 states that as of December 2010 the Chinese military had held forty-four joint military and training exercises with foreign counterparts.[7]

China has also increased its participation in joint naval activities and other naval deployments abroad for humanitarian purposes. In recent years it has held bilateral exercises with the navies of Australia, Canada, France, India, Pakistan, Thailand, the United

Kingdom, and the United States. Furthermore, in December 2008 China announced that it would cooperate with the multinational antipiracy force in the Gulf of Aden and deployed its first ships to the region. In September 2009 military officials from Australia and the United States announced that they would invite China to take part in trilateral military exercises, initially focusing on humanitarian assistance and disaster relief.[8] According to the March 2011 white paper, as of December 2010 the Chinese navy had completed a total of seven deployments to the Gulf of Aden area, involving eighteen ships, and provided protection for more than 3,100 ships under Chinese and foreign flags.[9] In 2010, the newly built naval hospital ship, whose Chinese name means "Peace Ark," undertook an eighty-eight-day humanitarian mission with stops in Africa and South Asia, the first such deployment for the Chinese navy.

This increased activity related to peace and stability operations, as well as increased humanitarian activity by the Chinese military, is driven by the broad motivations behind China's new security diplomacy over the past fifteen years. In addition, Chinese security forces benefit from practical experience gained through participation in different types of operations, overseas training opportunities, and close cooperation with other countries' forces.

Looking Ahead: Implications for Research and Policy

This brief overview does not suggest that there will be dramatic "new directions" in Chinese security policy anytime soon. But it does suggest a continuation in the trend that has been noted over the past ten to fifteen years, because of a solid appreciation by Chinese leaders that their country's key interests, and particularly its need to continue development trends at home, will increasingly require more constructive and active engagement abroad. This will include an increased need to understand and to approach more flexibly the nontraditional challenges that affect Chinese security.

If this assessment is correct, some of the next big questions for research and policy will be how and whether China will continue to pursue this relatively constructive approach to its foreign and security policy. Many impediments and uncertainties still lie ahead for this approach—the more assertive and abrasive policies and actions seen from China in 2010 and 2011 reflect this uncertainty.

First, an even more active role for China on the world stage has long been constrained by its own nearly unassailable maxims calling for the country to eschew international leadership and skirt controversial decisions in international affairs. Most often cited is Deng Xiaoping's well-known "twenty-four-character strategy" of the early 1990s, which continues to hold sway today. While its precise English translation is a matter of some debate, the overall thrust of Deng's admonition to Chinese leaders is to avoid taking the lead, keep a low profile, steer clear of trouble, and quietly focus on China's own capabilities. Deng's statement was later slightly modified and abbreviated to an eight-character slogan that remains a widely used guideline for internal party and governmental deliberations: *"tao guang yang hui, you suo zuo wei"* (keep a low profile and bide our time, while also making some contributions). Deng is also widely quoted as saying that "even if in the future China is a well-developed and strong nation, we should never seek to lead, never seek hegemony, never seek spheres of influence, never take sides with factions in world politics, never seek interference in the internal affairs of other states." While these strategic guidelines are debated in China, and some adjustments may be made to them, they serve as potent principles that will often restrain a more proactive Chinese foreign and security policy.

Second, China's willingness and ability to take part in bolder action on the international stage, unilaterally or with others, will continue to be limited by the pressing priorities of the country's internal and developmental problems, as well as by the inherent insecurity the leadership feels as it struggles to keep China's high-speed trajectory on course without losing control. Phenomenal dynamism, rapid transformation, and the steady boil of social and political unrest characterize the nation's domestic situation. Nationalism too is on the rise in China, with more and more "netizens" and elites calling on their leaders to be more assertive in leveraging the country's economic might toward securing Chinese interests and regaining China's "rightful" place among the world's most powerful nations. As the CCP frequently takes credit for China's rising status in recent decades, the Chinese leadership has become a victim of its own success and needs to proceed cautiously on the international stage.

The combination of remarkable economic growth, integration with a globalizing world, and the citizenry's increasing demands makes China a formidably complex country to govern. The leadership fears that leaving citizens' demands unchecked could lead to greater instability and a further loss of centralized sociopolitical control—hence the tough crackdowns across a wide spectrum within China over the last two years. Indeed, the remarkable social and political changes under way in much of the Arab world since early 2011 have encouraged an even tighter internal grip by Chinese authorities.

The Chinese leadership faces a difficult conundrum. On the one hand, increased engagement abroad is seen as an important pathway to help foster development at home. But at the end of the day, domestic challenges will always receive the topmost priority and may ultimately limit the willingness of China's leadership to engage actively the outside world. At a minimum, foreign policies will be shaped all the more by their impact on domestic stability.

Third, China's ability to be engaged more proactively on the international stage will also be constrained by the nature of its political system and governmental structure. Major decisions in China are taken through a deliberative and measured consensus-building process in which decisions once reached are difficult to change. As Deborah Seligsohn, a Beijing-based adviser for World Resources Institute, has noted, Chinese leaders are not truly "politicians" in the same sense as their counterparts in Western countries or, for that matter, in India, Brazil, or South Africa. Rather, they are bureaucrats, unaccustomed to on-the-fly deal making or the crafting of breakthroughs face to face with world leaders over the heads of their staffers, as was seen most clearly during the global climate summit in Copenhagen in 2009.

At the same time, important decisions in China are increasingly affected by a growing number of more powerful stakeholders, making consensus building all the more difficult and fragile, hence less open to adjustment by top leaders. The interests of government commissions and ministries, major financial and investment institutions, state-owned conglomerates, and municipal and provincial locales must all be taken into account.

Fourth, China's predominant focus on state-to-state relations will limit its ability to operate more flexibly in an increasingly complex and less state-centric world. In a world where many of the most important security actors and security challenges are nonstate or substate in nature, China will need to develop more sophisticated diplomatic tools to deal with them. It is not clear as yet how effective Beijing can be in such an environment. All governments face this problem in varying degrees, but among the world's major powers China may be the least experienced and most reluctant to engage nonstate actors.

Fifth, Chinese foreign and security policies will also be shaped—but probably not ultimately determined—by how Beijing interprets the actions and policies of its neighbors, especially those in East Asia, and particularly those allied with the United States. China likely will remain committed to reassuring its neighbors about its peaceful intentions and to avoiding an overt confrontation with the United States. Nevertheless, in recent years tensions between China and its neighbors, as well as in U.S.-China relations, have been on the rise, especially over maritime issues, such as freedom of the seas, territorial claims in the East China Sea and South China Sea, and U.S. military operations in the airspace and waters near China. The United States and others in the region must carefully calibrate their actions and policies with regard to these issues—at times even coordination would be advisable—in order to encourage continued constructive approaches from Beijing and to avoid inciting an assertive backlash or other potentially destabilizing and dangerous reaction. This will not be an easy balance and ensures that underlying tension in the region will remain a factor constraining an even more constructive Beijing on issues of concern in East Asia and beyond.

These constraints—in spite of positive advances in China's new security diplomacy over the past ten to fifteen years—will have implications for China's willingness and ability to meet rising international expectations that it should make a more constructive contribution to a range of nontraditional security challenges at the regional and global levels. Failure to close the expectations gap could not only increase tension between China and Western powers but further weaken the international community's ability to tackle a host of big problems: righting the global fiscal imbalance and achieving global economic recovery, mitigating climate change, ensuring development in the global South, addressing proliferation concerns in Iran and North Korea, resolving ongoing and looming regional conflicts (such as in Afghanistan), combating the spread of infectious diseases, tackling organized crime and illicit trafficking networks, and averting the fallout from weakening states like Yemen, Somalia, and the Democratic Republic of the Congo.

Accordingly, China's major international partners, including the United States, should have realistic expectations about Beijing's willingness and ability to be even more flexible and proactive in its foreign and security policy. Also, China's international partners will need to invest far more time and resources in understanding and interpreting Chinese domestic pressures, internal politics, and foreign-policy decision making. Debates and differing points of view are far more prominent and accessible in China today than in the past. Chinese leader Hu Jintao's 2009 emendation of Deng's original twenty-four-character slogan—Hu calls for an effort to try "more actively" to make contributions on the international scene—probably signals a recognition of the international community's growing expectations of China and is worth further exploration and elaboration.

In focusing on nontraditional security issues in official discussions with Beijing, Washington can accomplish three important goals. First, it can expand areas of common ground with Beijing and enlist Chinese assistance in combating regional and global challenges. Second, to the degree that Beijing addresses transnational threats emanating from within its own borders and seeks Washington's assistance in doing so, American and Chinese interests will benefit. Third, a focus on transnational challenges helps foster a broader, more internationalist, and more interdependent perspective in Chinese leadership circles, which in turn may constrain future unilateralist or nationalist tendencies as China grows stronger.

Overall, there lies a great deal of unexplored common ground between the United States and China on matters of nontraditional security. Given the fundamental motivations that will likely continue to drive China's security diplomacy and the increasing importance of nontraditional security challenges to the interests of China and the United States, it is reasonable to be cautiously optimistic that the two countries will devote greater resources to addressing jointly the transnational security problems they face.

Notes

1. White House, Office of the Press Secretary, "U.S.-China Joint Statement: Beijing, China," 17 November 2009, available at www.whitehouse.gov/.
2. "PRC: Liaowang Article Sees PRC's 'New Diplomacy' Stress on 'More Active' International Role," *Liaowang*, 11 July 2005, in Foreign Broadcast Information Service, CPP20050719000118, 19 July 2005.
3. One prominent group in Asia focusing on nontraditional security issues defines them thus: "Non-traditional security issues are challenges to the survival and well-being of peoples and states that arise primarily out of non-military sources. . . . These dangers are often transnational in scope, defying unilateral remedies and requiring comprehensive—political, economic, social—responses, as well as humanitarian use of military force." See *Consortium of Non-Traditional Security Studies in Asia*, www.rsis-ntsasia.org/.
4. This section draws in part from Bates Gill and Chin-hao Huang, *China's Expanding Role in Peacekeeping: Prospects and Policy Implications*, SIPRI Policy Paper 25 (Solna, Swed.: Stockholm International Peace Research Institute, November 2009).
5. International Committee of the Red Cross, *Annual Report 2007* (Geneva: May 2008).
6. "Defense Ministry Touts Deepened China-ASEAN Security Cooperation," Xinhua, 30 March 2009.
7. *China's National Defense in 2010* (Beijing: Information Office of the State Council, 31 March 2011), sec. IV.
8. "Military Chiefs Woo China: US, Australia Seek Joint Exercises to Ease Tension," *The Age*, 3 September 2009.
9. *China's National Defense in 2010*.

The PLA Navy's Gulf of Aden Mission as Capability Building against NTS Threats

You Ji

The study of nontraditional security (NTS) threats has become trendy in China in recent years. To the People's Liberation Army (PLA) this study is closely linked with another concept, military operations other than war (MOOTW), a concept that was once popular in U.S. military research but that was dropped in 2006.[1] Indeed, PLA efforts to cope with NTS threats are closely linked to the use of military forces in non-combat missions. In 2008, the General Staff Department set major categories of operations against NTS threats, in which eleven scenarios of action were envisaged. Almost all of them are designed to meet the challenge of NTS threats. International humanitarian assistance (IHA) operations are ranked highly among the General Staff Department's priorities. The categories of actions are operations related to emergency rescue, closing borders and suppressing border riots, counterterrorism, putting down domestic turmoil, engaging in international peacemaking, safeguarding China's maritime interests, and securing sea lines of communications (SLOCs) for Chinese commercial shipping. Today such operations are fully integrated into the "preparation for military struggle" of the PLA Navy (PLAN).[2]

On the other hand, although NTS threats—such as terrorism, natural disasters, and the structural shortfall of energy supplies, to name a few—have become routine for China, it is still the traditional security threats that preoccupy the minds of CCP and PLA leaders. Yet under a relatively benign assessment of China's overall external environment, Hu Jintao has ordered the PLA to strike a dialectical balance between actions against traditional and those against nontraditional threats, based on his call for the PLA to carry out multiple new missions in dealing with multiple security threats.[3] This has motivated the PLA to study and build capabilities enthusiastically to counter NTS threats.

The PLA Navy has factored NTS challenges into its planning for its overall transformation (整体转型) by adjusting its maritime strategy for the third time since 1987. It made significant revisions to meet the increased demand to secure China's strategic sea-lanes. Now, an open-ended range of economic interests prompts the PLAN to carry out a wider range of missions in an unlimited geographic setting.[4] Clearly PLAN transformation is still empowered by the "point" scenario (Taiwan). However, the most likely Chinese naval actions will for the foreseeable future be against NTS threats. Therefore, the PLA's efforts to enhance capabilities against NTS threats have been structured into its overall, capability-based transformation aimed at deterring conflict with major powers. Preparation for MOOTW is thus embedded in the PLA's preparation for real war, and this provides new dimensions for PLA modernization. The PLA Navy's Somalia counterpiracy operations are a good case study through which to analyze PLAN practices in dealing with NTS threats. The central question is how capabilities against both traditional and NTS threats are integrated under the guidance of war preparation for the decades ahead.

The PLA Navy's Multiple New Missions

Naval NTS operations are fundamentally externally oriented, whether for the purposes of humanitarian aid or for securing China's development interests. This is in contrast with other military services, whose NTS operations are largely for maintaining domestic political and social stability. Therefore, the PLAN takes China's MOOTW from land to sea with the following characteristics: fast to act, extending over long distances, having institutionalized operational procedures and force organization, and association with relevant civil sectors and other PLA services. China's capability to conduct overseas IHA operations is limited, and Beijing's low-profile diplomacy often proscribes PLA participation in these kinds of activities. PLAN IHA operations happen rarely. Therefore, the Gulf of Aden escort mission offered a good opportunity to catch up with the trend of

A Chinese navy air-cushioned landing craft (LCAC) deploys from the stern of a new amphibious assault ship during a recent deployment to the Gulf of Aden. Such advanced capabilities afford new opportunities for enhanced Chinese military roles in nontraditional security. LCACs, for example, are extremely useful for humanitarian assistance and disaster relief.

major powers. To this end, the PLAN has created an emergency command structure, a set of regulations and plans (预案) to direct these operations, and a high-powered integrated civil-military communication and transportation system.

MOOTW: The Naval Dimension. The PLAN's overseas tasks are diversified, ranging from peacemaking to humanitarian assistance (HA), SLOC protection, law enforcement in disputed areas, and the safeguarding of rights in the exclusive economic zone (EEZ). Therefore, China's maritime operations against NTS threats are oriented more toward potential combat than NTS operations within the homeland and thus tend to be more sensitive. The line between MOOTW and genuine combat action is sometimes narrow. As a result, the navy's effort toward MOOTW readiness is more closely tied to its overall war preparation. In answering Hu's declaration that "MOOTW has a special function in improving the PLA's war preparation and fighting capabilities," the navy is using MOOTW as a touchstone to evaluate its overall combat readiness.[5]

According to Vice Adm. Tian Zhong (田中), commander of the North Sea Fleet, naval NTS operations are designed to protect China's maritime interests, which can be clustered in three categories: core interests (sovereignty related, such as Taiwan); important interests (SLOC-safety related, such as oil transportation); and ordinary interests (such as maritime IHA). Functionally, naval NTS can be confrontational, especially against hostile encroachment of China's sovereignty. Such actions can be carried out through operations demonstrating Chinese naval presence, including maritime or aerial patrols and monitoring, tailing, and expelling vessels. The objective of these operations can be to test the adversary's bottom line, express China's security concerns, or display the navy's resolve. In a way, this is preventive military diplomacy, employing a relatively low level of "hard power." The next level of naval confrontation, short of armed conflict, is maritime deterrence, which is concretely embodied in such actions as purpose-specific naval exercises and targeted weapons tests. These naval activities are of a confrontational nature but are still short of war and are mounted against a political background that aims to generate heavy military pressure against hostile elements. In carrying out these actions it is important that the navy be firmly determined but also skillful in avoiding unwanted escalation. The PLAN should dare to show strength while at the same time exercising total process control.[6]

Additionally, the PLAN considers naval MOOTW to have specific features: geographic open-endedness that embraces the global reach of China's merchant ships; routinized operations (常态化), rather than one-off, or ad hoc, missions; close connection to the country's foreign-policy strategies and diplomatic needs; international cooperation (such as IHA operations with other naval powers); legitimization by proper international and domestic authorization; and selectivity, with careful cost-benefit evaluation based on the mission's value, material constraints, and possible global and domestic backlash. This is an incomplete list of guiding principles that any naval NTS operations would consider. As a novice in the MOOTW business, the PLAN has a lot more to learn before it can become a mature player.[7]

Enriching the PLAN's Maritime Strategy. The PLAN's unexpected participation in antipiracy and other NTS initiatives has enriched its maritime strategy. Adm. Liu Huaqing's 1987 blue-water maritime strategy aimed to make the PLAN a powerful regional navy.[8] To a certain extent, NTS threats to China's economic security have created new dimensions in the navy's strategic formulation, directing its geographic attention toward other oceans—for example, the Indian Ocean—twenty years earlier than originally thought. Necessary adjustments to Liu's original vision have been in order. These operations marked the beginning of a new approach for the PLAN, an approach that required it to undertake multiple missions to meet multiple threats. To this end the navy articulated a new conceptual goal, namely, to attain the capabilities of a regional navy. The expansion of the PLAN's mission set was driven by China's new geopolitical and geoeconomic imperatives.[9]

This notion guides the nature of the PLAN's transformation. It is strategic in several aspects. First, although the word "regional" refers geographically to China's adjacent waters (the East and South China Seas), in naval operational terms it covers "all maritime areas [全海域] that have a key bearing on China's national security and fall within the PLAN's effective reach."[10] Hence this is a flexible notion, with a specific concern for SLOC safety. Second, MOOTW serves as the linkage between the navy's long-term change and its immediate missions short of war. The idea of regional naval power no longer reflects simply a focus on combat capabilities vis-à-vis major naval adversaries. It deals also with NTS challenges, such as maritime terrorism and piracy. SLOC safety is thus integral to China's concept of "sea rights" that are crucially important to Beijing's emerging concept of sea power.[11] The idea of sea rights does not have any geographic limit; it legitimizes the PLAN's effort to achieve a degree of freedom of action in global waterways.[12] Third, the geographic openness has broadened China's priority of maritime defense, formerly understood as territorial defense. Now SLOC protection has gained great currency in the navy's strategic thinking.[13]

The concept offers a new perspective from which to analyze China's naval strategy. China's maritime interests far exceed the PLAN's geographic reach. Aside from the United States, the major powers confine their routine naval activities within regional settings in peacetime but are prepared if necessary to go anywhere to safeguard national interests. This offers a roadmap for China's naval transformation.[14] What it means is that the PLAN as a regional navy should have prescribed geographic limits for its usual activities but should possess sufficient power-projection capabilities to deal with hostile scenarios outside this geographic purview. Only with such capabilities can the PLAN claim the status of a true blue-water navy.[15] Therefore, naval capabilities are more important than a theoretical depiction of the geographic areas within which a navy should be present. Logically the notion of regional naval power unifies concepts of time, space, and capability. In the case of the PLAN, this involves the phases of its naval development out to 2020 (time), China's long sea-lanes (space), and the necessary hardware and software to achieve China's maritime objectives (capabilities).

The probability that the PLAN will engage a major power in a traditional sea battle is low. Yet NTS operations may occur with high frequency. Most NTS actions overseas are linked to SLOC challenges, which until recently had not been adequately addressed. Traditionally, China's anxiety concerning a major SLOC disruption was focused chiefly on the possibility of a naval blockade by major powers, with the probability of interdiction in the final segment of the shipping lanes to China—the western Pacific.[16] Today, however, threats mount in the early stage of shipment—such as the choke points in the Indian Ocean and beyond—and are often presented by nonstate actors. The PLAN's decision to undertake the Gulf of Aden escort operations reflects its doctrinal adjustment and the new requirement for force-structure developments to accommodate it. War preparation for the Taiwan scenario is significantly different from the protection of sea-lanes. For the former, amphibious capability is crucial; for the latter, forward presence and expeditionary fleets are essential. Combat doctrines, capability requirements, and weapons programs have to encompass both scenarios. While the former continues to enjoy priority, the PLAN has put more attention to and resources against SLOC challenges, which mainly take the form of NTS threats to China. These have led the navy into the deep oceans and helped it integrate its capability building, blue-water training, and increasing combat experience.

The PLAN realizes that a military response to a traditional challenge to SLOC security is largely a nonoption. The PLAN has no countervailing power against the superpower if the latter mounts a standard SLOC blockade against it. Also, naval operations are not the best solution to maritime NTS threats by nonstate actors. Diplomacy and international cooperation are the most cost-effective ways to manage such challenges, and military protection of SLOCs is always a last resort in Beijing's hierarchy of choices. Moreover, a major SLOC disaster is still a scenario more imagined than real, as long as the United States takes care of global SLOC security for itself and as long as its allies and littoral states cooperate in safeguarding regional waterways. China has benefited and continues to benefit from this multilateral mechanism.[17] Under such circumstances, China's SLOC strategy is two-pronged: seeking cooperation with the littoral states and accelerating naval building to acquire expeditionary capabilities. In the long term, the expeditionary fleets will be centered on aircraft carriers, but such capabilities will take a long time to become mature. Any immediate SLOC operations would fall to Chinese submarines, which could mount reverse deterrence against the enemy's maritime transport. The first is the main policy thrust and is being pursued proactively. The second is more of a hedging strategy, pursued in a low-key manner.[18]

This is by nature a kind of interim strategy to deal with the fact that the PLAN has no credible escort capability in the deep oceans. The ultimate goal of the navy is to possess its own escort fleets to protect its SLOCs from the Indian Ocean into China's domestic ports. Logically, Beijing hates to have Washington control its economic lifelines indefinitely. Building powerful high-sea fleets is the only way to minimize China's dependence on the United States for its SLOC security. Here, aircraft carriers are the symbol of the PLAN as a genuine blue-water navy. Yet the symbol is a symbol, not built for the purpose of achieving operational effectiveness against the powerful U.S. Navy. Therefore, the PLAN is unlikely to build carrier groups beyond a minimum number. The political leadership has not even made a decision to construct another carrier.[19] The PLAN will not enter an arms race with the U.S. Navy, but it will be firm in reducing American absolute naval superiority through increasingly capable asymmetric weaponry.

IHA Operations, SLOC Security, and PLAN Transformation

The PLA's mission in the Gulf of Aden is the first combat expeditionary mission since Zheng He's fleet sailed more than six hundred years ago.[20] As of late 2011, nine Chinese missions have participated in the operations, and twenty-seven warships have been dispatched; they have escorted 316 groups of 3,681 commercial ships and prevented eighty piracy attempts.[21] The response of other states to China's signal of willing participation in international security operations has been positive.[22]

An Opportunity Too Valuable to Miss. The Chinese antipiracy mission clearly has many motives. The nature of the piracy threat to human lives may qualify the Gulf of Aden operations as an international humanitarian move, and the PLAN prefers to define it as such.[23] But except for a few joint rescue exercises with foreign navies, the PLAN had never launched any true IHA operations, because of a lack of political will and a paucity of requisite capabilities. The navy does contribute to domestic HA and disaster-relief operations. For instance, in 2008 China conducted 1,784 maritime rescue operations, saving 19,595 lives, with a success rate of 97 percent.[24] But although PLA vessels occasionally picked up fishermen in the South and East China Seas during a storm, China's near seas were the farthest at which the PLAN conducted these operations, and that only on an ad hoc basis.

In the Gulf of Aden, the HA objective is not China's top concern, even though the PLAN conducts its operations there sincerely. Moreover, this mission is not primarily a SLOC action, as the best the pirates can do would be no more than a slight disruption to the navigation of a small number of merchant ships. The SLOCs there remain open, of course, despite the pirates' harassment. The PLAN mission has been justified by some as a move to improve the country's international image as a responsible global power. Yet the improvement may be only marginal, as piracy is not a major issue of concern for the majority of the world's population, and China's expeditions have generated instinctive worry among China's maritime neighbors. Indian concerns in particular may have somewhat offset any goodwill generated by Beijing's contributions to global SLOC security in the Indian Ocean.[25]

Therefore, what exactly motivated the PLA to mount such an expensive mission against a relatively minor threat? Clearly the PLAN's objectives are not confined to escort activities alone, as indicated by its enormous gains from the operations. In fact, the PLAN long sought such an opportunity. Soon after the first pirate attack on Chinese ships in the Gulf of Aden in May 2008, strategists in the PLAN Academic Research Institute (海军学术研究所) and the PLA National Defense University began discussing the feasibility of an escort mission there. After the completion of various new ship designs, the PLAN could not wait to test its new "teeth." A naval consensus on escort was discussed by Maj. Gen. Jin Yinan (金一南) in an interview broadcast in November 2008.[26] The Central Military Commission (CMC) quickly approved the navy's plan.[27] In the meantime, Chinese diplomats worked frantically to acquire an invitation from the Somali government for the escort mission. Beijing announced on 20 December 2008, only four days after UN Security Council (UNSC) Resolution 1851 was passed, that a three-ship detachment would be dispatched to the Gulf of Aden. The rapid decision process reflected the navy's eagerness to grab this opportunity, with unprecedented CMC support.

What is interesting is the very short interval between Beijing's announcement and the actual departure of the first task force ten days later. It is likely that preparation for the deployment predated the announcement, but it could not have begun too early, since the central decision was not made until late November 2008.[28] The preparation—such as the selection of combatants, study of the relevant information about a vast and strange ocean, logistical arrangements, and liaison with littoral states en route—is by nature time-consuming. This short period between decision and action is visible proof of the progress the PLAN has made in its ability to undertake rapid mobilization, maintain routine combat readiness, and provide material and information support for emergency action.

A Capability-Enhancement Mission. The Gulf of Aden mission is highly valuable for the PLAN's military transformation, given its lack of deepwater combat experience. Long-range overseas visits by major PLAN combatants have averaged four a year, but none of these have been combat deployments to test battle readiness. Indeed, the PLAN has sought a proper opportunity to leverage its blue-water power for a long time.[29] "Proper" here means a situation in which the sailors, as newcomers on the high seas, would not be subject to excessively tough battle conditions but would face encounters close enough to real engagements that they could taste an atmosphere of war. Clearly, high-seas counter-piracy operations were ideal as an "entry to the game."

Involving Personnel in a Combat Situation in the Deep Oceans. The PLAN has not been in a combat situation in the deep oceans since its last, small-scale clash with the Vietnamese in the South China Sea in 1988. While the Somalia escort is basically a police patrol, the PLAN is well prepared should the action evolve into armed conflict with pirates.[30] Indeed, exchanges of fire have already occurred on numerous occasions. For instance, by the end of the first two years of the mission, the escort fleet had engaged pirates twenty-one times with live fire and thereby saved thirty commercial ships.[31] What is more valuable for the sailors is the fact that they have to be on twenty-four-hour alert for the better part of four months during each deployment. On many occasions, for instance, unknown ships have suddenly appeared near the PLAN escorts, presenting a challenge to the sailors. Yang Wu (杨武), deputy head of the special operations unit embedded in the 9th Subfleet, disclosed that his sailors were under a three-second firing-readiness order.[32]

Moreover, it is common for helicopters to have to take off urgently at night and under difficult weather conditions. Unlike other major powers that have trained their troops in conditions of actual warfare, the PLAN has had to do it in simulation and in non-combat settings. The NTS mission in the Gulf of Aden tests the PLA's readiness, not only through real antipiracy actions but more so through exposing human resources to near-combat situations. For instance, the hours and sorties of helicopter pilots in a four-month rotation in the Gulf of Aden far exceed their whole year's flight time at home. This is especially true when, because of their increased rapid-reaction capability, the helicopters are hurriedly sent to dangerous spots. In the first mission the sailors stayed on board for about four months without touching land and under rather tough conditions.[33]

A Test of the Basic Composition of the Future Naval Task Group. Task forces of relatively small flotillas have been designated as the PLAN's basic deep-sea campaign formation in future wars.[34] These formations would be composed of a number of specialized warships, such as area-air-defense vessels, antisubmarine warfare (ASW) warships, supply ships, and submarines, most likely nuclear powered. These formations will be centered on aircraft carriers when carriers become operationally available in a decade or so. The PLAN's Somalia task group provides a basic form on which future expeditionary fleets can be organized. The first batch was an example. It consisted of Destroyers 169 and 171, as well as Replenishment Ship 887. Destroyer 169 is the flagship of the South Sea Fleet. It possesses the PLAN's best command, control, communications, computer, intelligence, surveillance, and reconnaissance (C4ISR) systems and most effective ASW capabilities, and it is specialized for sea-control missions. Destroyer 171 is one of the two surface combatants operating the Chinese analog to the U.S. Navy's Aegis system. Replenishment Ship 887 is the PLAN's largest and newest logistical vessel (twenty-two thousand tons), designed for long-range supply. These constituted the core components for the task force. Such ships, when joined with a few additional specialized warships, such as ASW and air-defense frigates and nuclear attack submarines, could form a standard deep-ocean maritime battle group.

Military Diplomacy and Cooperation. The PLAN ships in the Gulf of Aden have been in constant communication with other escort fleets, especially from Russia, the United States, NATO, and South Korea. They have thus gained good access to intelligence information, telecommunications, and radar signals shared by advanced navies.[35] This multilateral effort to safeguard the SLOCs helps the PLAN enhance international coordination and cooperation. Its regular contact, for instance, with Combined Task Force (CTF) 151 provides an opportunity to continue bilateral ties temporarily suspended because of U.S. arms sales to Taiwan. More practically, only through participation in international NTS operations will the PLA become competent in helping to formulate the rules of the game in the global arena. Moreover, the exchange of ship visits provides PLAN frontline commanders rare opportunities to learn how other navies handle near-combat situations. Since December 2009 the escort fleet has conducted over a dozen joint naval exercises with other navies in the Gulf of Aden.[36]

Managing Battlefield Situations. The most valuable benefit for the PLAN is the constant combat tests the escort fleet receives in dealing with questionable approaches by foreign warships. Some of these are innocent enough, but many of them are ill intentioned. For instance, the Chinese fleet has been followed by "unidentified spy planes, surface ships, and submarines" throughout the journey from Chinese waters to the Gulf of Aden. These vessels try to pick up the PLAN's communication signals, the pattern of coordination between ships in the formation, and their contact-management behavior. In fact, to Chinese naval officers the escort mission itself can be viewed as quasi electronic warfare, ASW warfare, and air-defense warfare. For instance, the PLAN fleet engages approaching contacts with its advance indication and warning (IW) systems to gather signals information. Such engagement is valuable in that it is "real combat," with which no confrontation between "Red" and "Blue" forces in an internal exercise can compare. It is "war without smoke," as it is called.[37] Moreover, the combat readiness of participating warships has been enhanced by the unprecedented challenge of long-range logistical supply, real-time C4ISR connection with PLAN headquarters in Beijing, and combat situations against hostile opponents. In short, the PLAN has benefited greatly from participation in the international efforts against the pirates.

Future Capability Building for NTS Operations

IHA and other forms of NTS operations have required a new, additional focus for the PLAN's weapons-development programs. Weak HA capability has been a "short board in the bucket." Although the Taiwan scenario still tops PLAN action plans, NTS operations like those in the Gulf of Aden may be the navy's primary concern at particular points in time and require specific, strengthened capabilities for IHA to cater to its immediate hardware and software demands.[38] This mission-led weapons development adds a new dimension to the PLAN's overall capability-led transformation and helps to fill in blanks in the naval arsenal. The following are selected key items in the navy's capability-enhancement efforts for future NTS missions.

Enhanced C4ISR Architecture. Currently the PLA and the navy do not have specialized command-and-control centers for NTS missions.[39] The navy's Gulf of Aden command model is typically the traditional one for a standard, limited, maritime regional war, a model that follows the naval headquarters–special detachment format.[40] For instance, both the CMC and naval headquarters have representatives in the forward command team of the escort fleet. This command model is appropriate for strategic operations, but as the Somalia mission is basically tactical and has become routine, a question has been raised as to whether it is necessary to place it under such centralized control. Clearly, once the rules of engagement are set, the commander of the escort mission could assume most responsibilities. This would improve command efficiency.

Enhancing C4ISR capability continues to enjoy priority as a development goal as the PLAN expands its global reach. But the Gulf of Aden mission is actually leading the way. The warships participating in the PLAN's Somalia operations are all capable of real-time vertical and horizontal communications—that is, with headquarters and among themselves—a key criterion for their selection for the mission. Also, the two-layer command chain—naval headquarters and the escort fleet—enables the ships to be on twenty-four-hour combat duty, with a seamless communications network in full readiness.[41] This sets the direction of technological advancement for the navy's future C4ISR improvement. For instance, the on-board satellite-based communications facilities will be integrated with the Chinese Beidou GPS. Data-link systems will be constantly upgraded in order to quicken the pace of reaction, improve IW in combat situations, and broaden the connectivity of hardware and software equipment. The goal is to make expeditionary warships capable of network-centric warfare against both traditional security threats and NTS challenges.

New Platforms for NTS Operations. As NTS operations are a relatively new task for the PLAN, the weapons-development programs have only recently factored in mission-specific requirements. The major surface combatants that have so far been deployed are, in a way, unnecessarily sophisticated for antipiracy missions and less than optimally effective for IHA. Rear Adm. Du Jingcheng (杜景臣), the commander of the first squadron, reported to the naval headquarters after returning home that the functional range of the weapons on board Destroyers 171 and 169 had been too narrow, poorly matching the needs of antipiracy operations in the Gulf of Aden. This revealed a large gap in the navy's inventory for multiple tasks.[42] Moreover, the large ships' operational cost was too high. Many of their facilities were fragile and not of much use, representing an enormous waste of resources. Rear Adm. Yin Zhuo (尹卓) raised the idea of building simplified Type 054 frigates to cater to IHA and antipiracy operations. These frigates would have a smaller displacement of three thousand tons, fewer weapons systems—such as missiles—and enhanced special equipment for HA and other NTS tasks. In order to cut cost, their construction standards could be set as half military, half civilian.[43] Yin's suggestion is in line with the PLA's new armament requirement for MOOTW. The importance of a dedicated inventory lies in the fact that NTS threats, such as Somali or Malaccan piracy, are long lasting. Cheaper warships may relieve the top-tier destroyers so the latter can concentrate on more traditional combat missions. Currently, most of the escorting ships in the mission are Type 054 frigates.

China has been especially weak in IHA capabilities, but this is now changing. One illustrative example concerns the PLAN's nonparticipation in the Southeast Asia tsunami rescue effort in December 2004, when its Type 886 hospital ship, the largest one in the world, and Type 071 amphibious ship (an LHA, twenty thousand tons) were both still under construction. Today the PLAN can undertake the IHA mission with much more confidence. Nonetheless, the PLA will remain selective in undertaking IHA, because of its high cost and China's diplomatic sensibilities. After all its major surface combatants have rotated through the mission and once its escorting ships have stayed for a decent period in the Gulf of Aden, it might be time for the PLAN to seek an "exit." Instead, deploying the hospital ship for IHA missions could be a low-budget move that achieves a solid humanitarian effect. It would also extend China's soft-power influence to a region that is sensitive about China's military activities. The two voyages of Hospital Ship 886, to Somalia and to Latin America, reflected this strategic calculus. Hospital Ship 886 is the flagship of a subfleet for emergent medical services. Its entry into service is seen as a major breakthrough in the PLAN's medical-support capability for blue-water operations.[44]

One alternative would be to turn an amphibious assault ship into a rescue platform in time of crisis. Yet, at the moment, the PLAN does not have a sufficient number of oceangoing amphibious ships. The Type 071 has filled a gap, but the navy needs at least a squadron of them to meet minimum requirements. The acquisition of large amphibious ships and helicopter carriers by the Japanese and the Koreans has stimulated the PLAN to seek similar capabilities that are good not only for expeditionary purposes but also for IHA missions. It can be expected that the navy's new phase of surface shipbuilding would make it a major task to construct up to five Type 071s and possibly three Type 081 LPHs as well.[45]

Seeking Forward Presence for Logistical Supply. The routinized Gulf of Aden operations exposed a serious weakness in the PLAN's blue-water expeditionary capabilities—the lack of forward presence for logistics. The crews of the first detachment never had a chance to rest on land during their four-month mission. Although the navy started to arrange port visits beginning with the second group, the sailors are permitted only one rest period on land. European sailors are allowed breaks on shore after just fifteen days at sea. This situation continues to stretch the physical endurance of PLAN sailors to the extreme. Moreover, the current mode of having a supply ship accompany the warships is much more expensive than port calls, and the PLA has only three large supply ships capable of sustained deep-ocean missions. This is why the replenishment ships *Weishanhu* and *Qiandaohu* have to accompany the flotillas repeatedly. That Japan acquired a base in Djibouti rekindled PLAN discussion about the desirability of having a forward foothold near Somalia.[46] Rear Adm. Yin Zhuo's remarks on the need for a forward base caused a stir among international defense analysts but were dismissed by the Ministry of Defense as unlikely.[47] Yet, interestingly, Yin seems to have received overwhelming public support.

Today, PLAN Gulf of Aden operations have become routinized, but logistical arrangements remain ad hoc. There is a mental gap in the minds of leaders between the foreign-policy need to convince the world that China's Gulf of Aden mission is not a step toward expansionism and a naval operational requirement for effective logistical support. The current solution requires Chinese sailors to pay a physical price for the mission. Rear Admiral Yin's thoughts reflect an emerging naval consensus that a more sensible logistical arrangement has to be found for the escort fleet. Col. Wu Fan made a good point in regard to the policy conservatism with regard to PLAN port visits. The argument against frequent port visits was based on a concern about possible negative responses from locals. However, the PLAN later discovered that the locals actually welcomed the Chinese sailors.[48] It is likely that some arrangements along this line will be made for the PLAN and that this will serve as a pattern for future Chinese IHA missions, especially those that last for lengthy periods. The question now is basically about the right timing to try this approach.[49]

Conclusion

NTS operations will be a permanent feature of the PLA's transformation. The Chinese navy's IHA operations will enjoy temporary emphasis, as is seen in the Gulf of Aden escort missions, and the Chinese fleet may even stay in the Gulf of Aden for a long time, because of the persistent nature of the piracy problem, as will the escort fleets of other major powers. This is why the operations have become routine. Yet the PLAN may not want to see its Somalia mission last for too long. It is a huge drain of scant resources and has low priority compared to war preparation. As other strategic directions—such as Taiwan in 2012—demand increased attention, calls for the PLAN to find an exit will become pressing.

On the other hand, the concept of multiple missions against multiple threats, including NTS threats, has become a part of the PLAN's overall transformation. This applies to the hardware and software development for dealing with NTS. The guiding principle is "enough but limited"—that is, exceeding what is required but not by much.[50] Yet as the PLAN's IHA missions will likely be carried out far from home and often in complicated international situations, the PLA Navy would prefer more than "just enough." It is clear that the PLAN's engagement of nontraditional security scenarios will serve its overall combat capabilities and that, by the same token, when its overall capabilities are enhanced, it will be better able to cope with NTS threats.

Notes

1. 涂炳林 and 张云胜 [Tu Binlin and Zhang Yunsheng], 非战争军事行动政治工作概论 [Outline on Political Work in MOOTW] (Beijing: Blue Sky, 2009), p. 7.

2. 于和平 [Senior Col. Yu Heping] et al., "论非战争行动财务保障能力建设的目标与任务" [On the Objective and Tasks of Capability Building for MOOTW], 军事经济研究 [Military Economic Studies], no. 8 (2008), p. 62.

3. David Lai, Andrew Scobell, and Roy Kamphausen, eds., *The PLA at Home and Abroad* (Carlisle, Pa.: U.S. Army War College, National Bureau of Asian Research and Strategic Studies Institute, 2010).

4. See You Ji, "Dealing with the Malacca Dilemma: China's Effort to Protect Its Energy Supply," *Strategic Analysis* 31, no. 3 (September 2007), pp. 467–89.

5. 李世明 [Gen. Li Shimin], "多样化军事任务战略思想的时代价值和实践要求" [The Epoch-Making Value and Practical Demand to Fulfill the Multiple Military Missions], 中国军事科学 [Chinese Military Science], no. 5 (2008), p. 62.

6. 田中 [Adm. Tian Zhong], "海军非战争军事行动的特点、类型及能力建设" [The Special Characteristics, Types and Capability Construction for Naval MOOTW], 中国军事科学 [Chinese Military Science], no. 3 (2008), p. 27.

7. Summaries of interviews with naval researchers by the author in Beijing, 2010.

8. 刘华清 [Adm. Liu Huaqing], 刘华清回忆录 [The Memoirs of Liu Huaqing] (Beijing: PLA Publishing House, 2004).

9. 刘一健 [Capt. Liu Yijian], 制海权与海军战略 [The Command of the Sea and Naval Strategy] (Beijing: PLA National Defense Univ. Press, 2004), p. 233.

10. 孙景平 [Col. Sun Jingping], "新世纪新阶段海上安全战略断想" [Thoughts on Maritime Strategy in the New Period in the New Century], 中国军事科学 [Chinese Military Science], no. 6 (2008), p. 74.

11. 张文木 [Zhang Wenmu], "Sea Power and China's Strategic Choice," *China Security* (Summer 2006), p. 23.

12. Liu, *Command of the Sea and Naval Strategy*, p. 25.

13. Andrew Erickson and Lyle Goldstein, "Gunboats for China's New 'Grand Canals'? Probing the Intersection of Beijing's Naval and Oil Security Policies," *Naval War College Review* 62, no. 2 (Spring 2009), pp. 43–76.

14. Liu, *Command of the Sea and Naval Strategy*, p. 230.

15. 张序三 [Adm. Zhang Xusen], "试论未来海上战役的指导思想" [On the Guiding Principle of Our Campaign Tactics in Future Wars], in 通向胜利的探索 [Exploring the Ways toward Victory] (Beijing: PLA Publishing House, 1987), p. 1000.

16. Ibid., p. 984.
17. 胡仕胜 [Hu Shisheng], "印度洋与中国海上安全" [The Indian Ocean and China's Maritime Security], in 扬明杰 [Yang Mingjie ed.], 海上通道安全与国际合作 [SLOCs Security and International Cooperation] (Beijing: Current Events Press, 2005), p. 353.
18. You, "Dealing with the Malacca Dilemma," pp. 467–89.
19. Chen Bingde, speaking at a joint news conference with Admiral Mullen, Beijing, 11 July 2011.
20. "挑战中开创中国海军新历史" [Creating New History for the PLAN], 人民海军报 [People's Navy], 23 December 2009.
21. Chinese Ministry of Defense website, www.mod.gov.cn
22. Andrew Erickson and Justin Mikolay, "Welcome China to the Fight against Pirates," U.S. Naval Institute *Proceedings* 135, no. 3 (2009).
23. 沈浩 [Shen Hao], "中国海军作战部长答本刊记者问" [Naval Operations Chief Answers Questions from This Journal], 当代海军 [Modern Navy], no. 2 (2009), p. 16.
24. Ibid., p. 15.
25. James Holmes and Toshi Yoshihara, "Is China a Soft Naval Power?" *China Brief*, no. 8 (August 2009).
26. Jin Yinan, radio interview, 26 December 2008, available at cn.chinareviewnews.com/crn.
27. "中国海军为国家利益挺进深蓝" [The PLAN Explores Blue Water for the National Interests], 中国新闻周刊 [Chinese News Weekly], 1 February 2009.
28. In late November 2008 *People's Navy* started to publish articles arguing why the PLAN should dispatch warships to the Gulf of Aden. This development indicated a CMC decision on the escort.
29. For instance, naval scholars debated whether to send ships to observe U.S.-led Iraqi operations. To their disappointment, the central decision was no.
30. 彭光谦 [Maj. Gen. Peng Guangqian], quoted on Phoenix TV, 4 January 2009.
31. Xinhua, 22 December 2010.
32. "Comprehensive Combat Drills Conducted by the 9th Escort Fleet," *PLA Daily*, 18 August 2011.
33. Ibid.
34. 陈访友 [Chen Fangyou], 海军战役学教程 [Textbook for Naval Campaign Theory] (Beijing: PLA National Defense Univ. Press, 1991), p. 164.
35. "中国海军护航行动大事记" [The Major Events in the Two Years of PLAN Escort in the Gulf of Aden], PRC Ministry of National Defense website, www.mod.gov.cn.
36. See, for example, "中俄首次联合护航行动意义重大" [The Significance of the First Sino-Russian Joint Escort], 人民海军报 [People's Navy], 23 October 2009.
37. Views expressed at the PLA Navy's "Naval Symposium to Mark the Two-Year Anniversary of the Somalia Escort," Beijing, 20–21 December 2010.
38. Tian, "Special Characteristics, Types and Capability Construction for Naval MOOTW," p. 28.
39. 何雷 [Maj. Gen. He Lei], "大力提高非战争应急军事行动指挥能力" [Greatly Enhancing the PLA's Command Ability in the Conduct of Emergent MOOTW], 科学时报 [Science Times], 3 March 2010.
40. Speech by the naval representative to the PLA Military Operations Other than War Conference, Beijing, 6 September 2011.
41. Ibid.
42. 人民海军报 [People's Navy], 24 February 2010. Du Jingcheng has received several promotions since then. He is now chief of staff of the navy and a candidate to become commander of the navy.
43. 新华社 [New China News Agency], 25 December 2009.
44. 姜中岳 [Jiang Zhingyue], "医院船的国际法解读" [An International Law Explanation Regarding Hospital Ships], 人民海军报 [People's Navy], 25 August 2009.
45. 新浪军事网 [sina.net], accessed 15 March 2010.
46. "日本海军海外建基地引人深思" [The Deep Thought Aroused by Japan Setting Up an Overseas Naval Base], 人民海军报 [People's Navy], 11 November 2009.
47. Yin Zhuo, interview with Sun Li, *China Radio International*, 26 December 2009.
48. Col. Wu Fan (speech to Australian Defense College, 25 March 2010).
49. Sun, "Thoughts on Maritime Strategy in the New Period in the New Century," p. 81.
50. 冯梁 [Senior Col. Feng Liang], "关于稳定中国海上安全环境的战略思考" [Strategic Thinking on Stabilizing China's Maritime Security Environment], 中国军事科学 [Chinese Military Science], no. 5 (2009), p. 66.

The PLA (Re-)Discovers Nontraditional Security

Andrew Scobell and Gregory Stevenson

In recent years the People's Republic of China (PRC) has become increasingly concerned with nontraditional security threats. Not surprisingly, greater focus on nontraditional security by China's political leaders has been followed by growing attention to this category of threats by the Chinese People's Liberation Army (PLA). What is driving Beijing's interest in so-called nontraditional security challenges, and what has this meant for the PLA? What is the significance of this turn to nontraditional security for the PLA? What does it mean for the United States?

Before beginning an analysis of what is driving China's turn toward nontraditional security challenges, it is important to try to pin down exactly what Chinese political and military leaders mean by "nontraditional security." There seems to be no readily available single formal or widely accepted Chinese-government or PLA definition of nontraditional security.[1] Different academic and official publications give examples of what constitutes nontraditional security threats (非传统安全威胁) or nontraditional security issues (非传统安全问题). According to the 2008 defense white paper, nontraditional security threats include terrorism, natural disasters, economic insecurity, and information insecurity. Interestingly, "separatist forces" are particularly singled out as significant "threats to China's unity and security." For China, separatism is synonymous with terrorism and extremism—the three are grouped together and are dubbed "the three evils."[2] Separatism is identified in the sentence immediately prior to this laundry list of nontraditional security threats in the 2008 defense white paper.[3] Previous white papers discussed nontraditional security challenges. The term "nontraditional security" was first used in the 2002 iteration; the threats mentioned in the document were terrorism, transnational crime, environmental degradation, and drug trafficking. The 2004 iteration added the following nontraditional issues: "energy security, financial security, and epidemic diseases." Other analysts have included other threats such as piracy, proliferation of weapons of mass destruction (WMD), illegal immigration, and transnational crime, as well as "Internet hacking, the shortage of water resources, fishery conflicts, [and even] traffic congestion."[4] The 2011 triple Japanese tragedy of an earthquake, tsunami, and nuclear meltdown only served to highlight the potential for such nontraditional security threats on Chinese soil.

While there is no common definition, there are at least four key characteristics of nontraditional security that most Chinese scholars, analysts, and strategists agree on. First, nontraditional security threats are transnational in scope, with both domestic and international components; as a result, the "line between internal and external is blurred."[5] Second, Chinese researchers consider nontraditional security threats to be extremely volatile and unpredictable; Beijing is especially unnerved by them.[6] Third, nontraditional security challenges are "nonmilitary threats"; indeed, they "go beyond the military sphere" and manifest themselves in political, economic, or social domains.[7] Fourth, nontraditional security threats are often "interwoven and interactive [交织互动] with traditional security threats."[8]

Back to the Future?

In a sense this attention to nontraditional military missions represents a return to the PLA's traditions of functioning as more than just a fighting force. It was Mao who admonished the soldiers of the worker and peasant army to be more than just war fighters. In addition to preparing to wage armed struggle, they were charged with being economically and educationally productive, as well as with pitching in to assist whenever and wherever they were needed. According to military writer Song Puxuan, "For a long time now, we have only been accustomed to taking nonwar military action as something we should do as our duty and for no reward, as a means of dealing with special situations, and as a friendly means of participation, and . . . [have not] resolved to bring it into the domain of skills. [Moreover], theoretical research [in nonwar military action] is relatively lagging, and in some aspects is 'blank.'"[9]

In the twenty-first century, three main roles have been identified for the PLA. First and foremost, the primary function of China's military is war fighting. This entails being ready for combat operations. Since 2002 the main war-fighting scenario for the PLA has been identified as "local war in conditions of informatization" (see the figure).

Evolution of PLA Doctrine

2002	Local War in Conditions of Informatization introduced, and nontraditional security concept highlighted
2004	New Historic Missions identified
2006	Diversified Military Tasks outlined
2008	Military operations other than war articulated

In fact, this is an extremely generic scenario that encompasses a wide variety of contingencies, including almost any specific scenario less than all-out war—in other words, any conflict requiring less than full national military mobilization. "Informatization" (信息化) is used to mean leveraging new technology in a number of ways: building networked command-information systems, joint operations command-and-control systems, battlefield information support, and logistical and equipment-support information systems.

The second function of China's military is deterrence. In contemporary Chinese strategic thought, making good on the PLA's deterrent function encompasses a wide variety of activities, including rhetoric and action.[10] The third function is to perform "diversified military tasks" (多样化军事任务). This third function, in its current formulation, is relatively new and was only explicitly identified in 2006. The Diversified Military Tasks are a clarification of the New Historic Missions outlined by President Hu Jintao in December 2004. However, the prefix "new" is really a misnomer, because none of these missions are really new for the PLA.[11] The New Historic Missions are an important restatement of existing missions. The PLA has always had the missions of defending the Chinese Communist Party (CCP) and supporting economic development.

The 2008 defense white paper states that the Diversified Military Tasks have the New Historic Missions as their "focus," with Local War in Conditions of Informatization as the "core." The New Historic Missions charge the PLA with maintaining "maritime, space and electromagnetic space security"—representing a significant expansion of military responsibilities—as well as conducting military operations other than war (MOOTW). The phrasing clearly establishes a hierarchy of importance about these duties.

Drivers

There are a number of drivers behind this growing attention to nontraditional security concerns. The primary impetus comes from CCP leaders. Fundamentally, this attention is motivated by the insecurity of China's ruling elite, driven by fears regarding the natures and scopes of the most dangerous threats to their security. At the same time, China's leaders are looking to cement ties between the party and army, and Beijing is determined to promote a positive and benign image internationally.

First, Beijing's embrace of globalization since the late 1990s has heightened alarm over the serious challenges that globalization poses to China as a country and to CCP rule. According to one scholar, "Since the 1990s, China has been frequently hit by nontraditional security threats." While such threats "are not new for China," their magnitude and severity "have remarkably increased thanks to globalization and liberalization."[12] While traditional security threats have diminished or at least become less urgent in the eyes of Chinese leaders, nontraditional security threats loom larger and more pressing. According to Gen. Xiong Guangkai, such twenty-first-century events as 9/11, severe acute respiratory syndrome (SARS), and the Southeast Asian tsunami underscore that "nontraditional security threats are becoming ever more prominent."[13] The heightened awareness of nontraditional security threats coincided with the publication in 1999 of the controversial book *Unrestricted Warfare*. Perhaps, rather underscoring the worrisome threat of a rising China, the book is better understood as highlighting concerns among many Chinese over their own country's increasing vulnerability to nontraditional security threats.[14]

Beijing is fearful of globalization, although it has concluded that China has no choice but to embrace it if the country is to perpetuate the economic boom and continue its great-power rise. A series of systemic shocks in the late 1990s—the Asian financial crisis, the audacious protest by Falun Gong followers outside the inner sanctum of the CCP in Beijing, the accidental U.S. bombing of the Chinese embassy in Belgrade, American reluctance to support swift Chinese admission to the World Trade Organization (WTO), and the inflammatory rhetoric of Taiwanese president Lee Teng-hui—forced Beijing to reassess its strategy and priorities. But in the end, CCP leaders decided that retreat was not an option.[15] As a result the PRC security establishment, including the armed forces, was directed to deal with a wide array of nontraditional security threats both at home and abroad.

Second, the attention to nontraditional security missions is an important means by which to stress the links between the CCP and the PLA. The army belongs to the party. Beyond this effort is an ongoing effort to conflate the party and the state.[16] A close look at the New Historic Missions reveals that this is so. The army's most important mission is to defend the party. Attention to nontraditional security missions is a key way to highlight the traditional bond between the CCP and the PLA. Moreover, attention to nontraditional security missions highlights the PLA's central role in China's "peaceful development," with both key internal and external dimensions. The PLA's missions go beyond defending China's sovereignty with armed force if necessary. The PLA is also a force for good—helping Chinese people recover from natural disasters and promoting the cause of world peace, wearing the blue helmets of the United Nations. Through these efforts, Beijing strengthens the centrality of the PLA and the supreme authority of the CCP within the nation and the state.

Third, the focus on nontraditional security missions is packaged in such a way as to make it part and parcel of Hu Jintao's personal contribution to military doctrine. The New Historic Missions were formally announced by Hu in December 2004 in an address to the Central Military Commission.[17] Each successive paramount Chinese political leader is expected to make a noteworthy contribution to strategic thought. Hu Jintao is now associated with the New Historic Missions and "scientific development."

Fourth, the attention to nontraditional security missions is part of a larger Beijing effort to stress that other countries do not need to fear China's growing military power. This is a concerted public-relations campaign to focus on noncombat missions and promote them as areas for cooperation. PLA attention to nontraditional security threats has been emphasized to foreign audiences. For example, during Gen. Xu Caihou's visit to the United States in October 2009 he repeatedly emphasized the nontraditional security challenges that have confronted the PLA in recent years. He particularly emphasized the military's efforts in dealing with domestic challenges, including humanitarian assistance and disaster relief in responding to the May 2008 earthquake in Sichuan Province.[18]

The PLA's Response to Nontraditional Security Challenges

Transnational challenges since the late 1990s have heightened Beijing's concern over nontraditional security threats. Ultimately, the response of China's armed forces has been to incorporate nontraditional security challenges into doctrine under the rubric of MOOTW.

Placing the PLA at the forefront of countering nontraditional security threats is a way to provide impetus for military modernization in peacetime. Moreover, the absence of an imminent threat of armed conflict lessens Beijing's sense of urgency driving the double-digit annual growth in defense spending. However, an unprecedented period of sustained prosperity in post-1949 China means that there are substantial party-state resources available for military modernization.

Especially with the improvement in relations across the Taiwan Strait since the election of Kuomintang presidential candidate Ma Ying-jeou in March 2008, the likelihood of a

Chinese capabilities for expeditionary military operations are rapidly increasing, as suggested by this aerial deployment of an armored personnel vehicle. This advance in capabilities will serve international security, especially if the PLA continues its new focus on nontraditional security and begins to operate more closely with other militaries, including that of the United States.

confrontation between Beijing and Taipei has diminished considerably. If the PLA can demonstrate its usefulness and value to the party, the people, and the nation in times of peace, that is strong justification for continued defense outlays. Since savvy military leaders know the mantra "Policy is what gets funded," support of policy is merely smart politics. As a result there has been a noticeable trend in hyping by soldiers from various services the important roles their particular branches play in nontraditional security missions.

Within the PLA the attention to nontraditional missions has been met with mixed feelings, varying according to the particular constituency. Among many in the military's higher echelons there is a feeling that China is unlikely to face a war in the near term.[19] With this assessment comes a willingness to focus attention on non-war-fighting missions. The caveat, of course, is that war fighting should not be ignored and that nontraditional security missions should not detract from the PLA's combat readiness.

In addition, the focus on nontraditional security threats and the PLA's efforts to address them are seen as excellent ways to refute the "China threat theory." Beijing is unhappy with fears voiced abroad that its growing military power poses a threat to its neighbors and other countries. Chinese leaders recognize that their country confronts a significant public-relations problem where military modernization is concerned, although it is very rarely explicitly or bluntly addressed. Adm. Tian Zhong, concurrently commander of the Northern Fleet and deputy commander of the Jinan Military Region, alludes to this problem in a 2008 article in a prominent Chinese military journal. The objective of the PLA Navy, Tian writes, is not solely to enhance its operational capabilities but also to serve a soft-power function: "The navy must strengthen its management of weaponry, display our country's ability in operations to defy the might of other navies, *and display the image of a peaceful rise* and the image of a mighty and civilized military."[20]

Moreover, the recent visible attention to MOOTW appears largely targeted at foreign audiences. One illustration of this is that the MOOTW acronym is prominently displayed, along with a peace symbol, on the English-language web page of the Ministry of National Defense (MND), while neither the English acronym nor 非战争军事行动 is used on the Chinese-language page. The MND's Chinese-language website simply uses the term 军事行动 (military operations).[21]

Additionally, some in the PLA may view military efforts aimed at nontraditional security threats as a way to acquire useful operational experience in absence of war. Of course, MOOTW cannot simulate combat operations, but they can nevertheless provide valuable training opportunities at a time when actual war-fighting experience is not possible. The U.S. armed forces are able to capitalize on the Long War and on ongoing and recent combat operations in Afghanistan and Iraq to gain valuable operational experience.

Operations in peacetime are no substitute, but some missions can offer significant real-world experience beyond mere training exercises. For the ground forces, participation in multinational peacekeeping operations in trouble spots around the world has proved immensely educational. For the PLA Navy, the antipiracy mission in the Gulf of Aden since late 2008 has provided a wealth of operational experience for Chinese mariners and has forced the PLA Navy to confront the challenges of projecting and sustaining naval power thousands of miles from the flotilla's home port.

Some analysts may downplay the significance of the operational experience gained by the PLA in dealing with nontraditional security threats. In the post–Cold War era, American military personnel have frequently been dismissive of the value that MOOTW experience provides to military units. This thinking, while certainly present within the PLA leadership, appears much less entrenched than it is among the leaders of the U.S. armed forces.[22] This is because Chinese soldiers, sailors, and airmen have not had any significant combat experience in decades.

In lieu of firsthand war-fighting experience, the PLA closely watches the combat operations of other armed forces. U.S. military capabilities in C4ISR are what Chinese soldiers aspire to and have been seeking to acquire. But the PLA has had no opportunity to test its evolving infrastructure and networks or to develop doctrine in order to integrate these systems in actual wartime operations.

The closest approximation to this kind of experience for the PLA is MOOTW. Thus, this experience is far more valuable for Chinese military personnel than it would be for their American counterparts. The PLA can make relatively larger gains from such experience than the American military might; more importantly, an increase in MOOTW may give the PLA experience more closely approximating that of its regional counterparts, such as the armed forces of Japan, South Korea, and India. The PLA has dealt with the daunting challenges of moving forces in adverse weather conditions when normal modes of transportation are unavailable or have been disrupted (e.g., the 2008 Wenchuan earthquake and snow emergency), supporting naval flotillas as far afield as the Gulf of Aden, and gaining experience, as PLA units conduct peacekeeping operations in such foreign climes as Africa.

The navy is perhaps better poised than the PLA air or ground forces to surge ahead on the crest of the nontraditional-security wave. Twenty-first-century concerns about piracy, terrorism, and threats to energy security and trade seem to favor a greater role for maritime forces. In fact, the PLA Navy seems to be the service branch most enthusiastic about MOOTW and best positioned and organized to exploit the concept for service interests. The navy has sought to highlight the central contribution that sea power can make in countering the multiple nontraditional security threats confronting

China. Admiral Tian began his 2008 article with the following lead-in: "The 17th Party Congress Report states: 'Raise military capabilities to deal with many different security threats, and accomplish diversified military tasks'; [moreover, the report] emphasizes in international relations managing 'mutual trust, strengthening cooperation, strengthening peaceful means but not war methods to solve international disputes.' The Navy can conduct strategic, comprehensive, and international military duties in vast maritime expanses to perform the New Historic Missions." Tian touted the "special characteristics" of the naval dimensions of MOOTW and the capabilities required.[23]

Moreover, the PLA Navy is stressing the importance and relevance of naval modernization to enhancing its ability to manage China's nontraditional security threats. Rear Adm. Zhang Huachen, deputy commander of the East Sea Fleet, recently told the Xinhua News Agency, "With the expansion of the country's economic interests, the navy wants to better protect the country's transportation routes and the safety of our major sea lanes. In order to achieve this, the Chinese navy needs to develop along the lines of bigger vessels with more comprehensive capabilities."[24]

Implications for the United States

For the United States, China's heightened interest in and concern about nontraditional security threats provide valuable opportunities for expanding military-to-military cooperation. There has already been cooperation in such areas as search-and-rescue exercises, but there is still enormous untapped potential. This engagement will allow each side to learn more about the other and build basic but important levels of mutual understanding, confidence, and trust. However, while the successful U.S. operation to neutralize Osama Bin Laden carried out in Pakistan in mid-2011 might appear a promising entrée into enhancing counterterrorism cooperation between the United States and China, this is not necessarily so. The operation was very impressive in Chinese eyes, but it also highlighted the capabilities of the U.S. military to undertake a similar operation inside any country in the world, including China. For China's civilian and military leaders, the operation itself and what appeared to be complete American disregard for the sovereignty and territorial integrity of another country were actually quite alarming and disconcerting. Meanwhile, in the United States, the China angle of the Bin Laden operation focused on reports that China had been permitted by Pakistan to examine the stealth technology of the U.S. helicopter that had had to be abandoned at the scene.[25] Additionally, monitoring PLA initiatives and operations dealing with a host of nontraditional security challenges offers key opportunities to learn about evolving operational capabilities.

Conclusion

The PLA has rediscovered its tradition of nontraditional security missions. Nontraditional security threats have loomed larger than traditional ones during the past decade. At least since the 1990s, the CCP leadership has decided it has no choice but to embrace globalization. The PLA has been grappling, particularly since the mid-2000s, with the task of finding an appropriate response. In wrestling with MOOTW, Chinese soldiers have pondered in very concrete terms the roles that the military can realistically play in countering nontraditional security challenges. The CCP, meanwhile, has used this element domestically to stress the sacred link between the party and the army and, externally, to emphasize China's peaceful rise and the PLA's role as a cooperative force for good in the world.

Notes

1. According to Susan L. Craig, "there is no formal agreed-upon definition" of nontraditional security in China. See Craig, *Chinese Perceptions of Traditional and Nontraditional Security Threats* (Carlisle, Pa.: U.S. Army War College, Strategic Studies Institute, March 2007), p. 101.

2. See Andrew Scobell, "Terrorism and Chinese Foreign Policy," in *China Rising: Power and Motivation in Chinese Foreign Policy*, ed. Yong Deng and Fei-ling Wang (Lanham, Md.: Rowman & Littlefield, 2005), pp. 305–24.

3. 2008年中国的国防 [*2008 nian Zhongguo de guofang*] [China's National Defense in 2008] (Beijing: Information Office of the State Council, January 2009), p. 6.

4. See Shanghai academic Guo Xuetong's list cited in Craig, *Chinese Perceptions of Traditional and Nontraditional Security Threats*, p. 103.

5. Craig, *Chinese Perceptions of Traditional and Nontraditional Security Threats*, p. 104. See also Song Puxuan, "Conscientiously Improve the Ability to Complete Diverse Military Tasks," *Liberation Army Daily*, 30 May 2008 (Internet version, trans. Open Source Center).

6. Craig, *Chinese Perceptions of Traditional and Nontraditional Security Threats*, p. 104.

7. Ibid., p. 103.

8. *China's National Defense in 2008*, p. 6.

9. Song, "Conscientiously Improve the Ability to Complete Diverse Military Tasks."

10. Andrew Scobell, "Discourse in 3-D: The PLA's Evolving Doctrine, circa 2009," in *The PLA at Home and Abroad: Assessing the Operational Capabilities of China's Military*, ed. Roy Kamphausen, David Lai, and Andrew Scobell (Carlisle Barracks, Pa.: U.S. Army War College, Strategic Studies Institute, forthcoming).

11. The authors have benefited from the insights of Paul H. B. Godwin.

12. Yu Xintian, quoted in Craig, *Chinese Perceptions of Traditional and Nontraditional Security Threats*, p. 104.

13. Craig, *Chinese Perceptions of Traditional and Nontraditional Security Threats*, p. 101.

14. 乔良, 王湘穗 [Qiao Liang and Wang Xiangsui], "超限战：两个空军大校对全球化时代战争与战法的想顶" [Unrestricted Warfare: The Pontifications of Two Air Force Senior Colonels on War and War Fighting in the Age of Globalization] (Beijing: PLA Literature, 1999).

15. David M. Finkelstein, *China Reconsiders Its National Security: The Great Peace and Development Debate of 1999* (Alexandria, Va.: December 2000).

16. See Andrew Scobell, *China's Use of Military Force: Beyond the Great Wall and the Long March* (Cambridge, U.K.: Cambridge Univ. Press, 2003), pp. 63–64.

17. Daniel M. Harnett, *Toward a Globally Focused Chinese Military: The New Historic Missions of the Chinese Armed Forces* (Alexandria, Va.: CNA, 2008).

18. Gen. Xu Caihou, vice chairman, Central Military Commission, People's Republic of China (address at the Center for Strategic and International Studies, Washington, D.C., 26 October 2009), personal communications, and available at www.mod.gov.cn/.

19. Author conversations with Chinese military researchers in 2008 and 2009.

20. 田中 [Tian Zhong], "海军非战争军事行动的特点、类型及能力建设" [Special Characteristics, Categories, Capabilities of Naval Military Operations Other than War], 中国军事科学 [China Military Science], no. 3 (2008), p. 26 [emphasis supplied].

21. See www.mod.gov.cn, website of the Ministry of National Defense.

22. See Scobell, "Discourse in 3-D."

23. Tian, "Special Characteristics, Categories, Capabilities of Naval Military Operations Other than War," p. 25.

24. Quoted in Edward Wong, "Chinese Military Seeks to Extend Its Naval Power," *New York Times,* 24 April 2010, p. A3.

25. On the Chinese reaction to the U.S. operation, see, for example, Pan Guoping, "US Action Violates International Law," *China Daily,* 19 May 2011, online in English, transmitted by Open Source Center, CPP20110519968043.

Issues in the Transformation of China's Engagement with International Peacekeeping

Pang Zhongying

Since 1990, China has been taking part in UN peacekeeping operations with its noncombat military forces and civilian police.[1] China's increasing support to international peacekeeping is a major driving force of the great transformation of international peacekeeping in the twenty-first century. China's peacekeeping role can be understood as Beijing's early experiment in undertaking more international responsibilities and even the benign projection of power by a rising nation.

Peacekeeping has become a priority in Beijing's foreign policy. As an expression of China's attachment of great importance to the peacekeeping issue in its foreign policy since 1998, *China's National Defense,* the annual white paper, views peacekeeping as an important part of China's "international security cooperation." China's "low key" foreign policy of "noninterventionism," adopted after the end of the Cold War, tried to avoid entanglement in the world's crises and troubles, but participation in peacekeeping causes China actually to face the challenge of the others' "internal" conflicts.

Participation in peacekeeping is one path for China's use of newly obtained national power. No doubt, although many problems have arisen in the process of China's economic development and modernization, China's national power has been steadily rising. China is gradually adapting to evolving peacekeeping norms and rules in the era of "second-generation peacekeeping." Its attitudes toward peacekeeping have been changing according to changed "external" circumstances and demands.

The reach of China's peacekeeping engagements and operations today is truly global. At least three Chinese ministries of the central government have been responsible for engagement with international peacekeeping: Foreign Affairs (foreign policy on peacekeeping), Defense (military peacekeepers), and Public Security (police peacekeepers). China has now become a major supplier of quality peacekeepers. As a "factory" for producing peacekeepers or as a global public good for international peacekeeping cooperation, China has established two training centers: the Beijing-based Defense Ministry's Peacekeeping Center, opened in June 2009, and the China Peacekeeping CIVPOL [UN Civilian Police] Training Center (CPCTC), established in August 2000 in the Beijing suburb of Langfang. The Langfang center is considered the largest and most modernized peacekeeping base in the international community, equipped mainly on the basis of China's "own innovations and researches."[2] In addition, a new question of a capacity divide may emerge: China's relatively better trained and equipped peacekeepers sharply contrast with what some analysts have warned are "relatively poorly equipped UN troops from the traditional peacekeeping nations," such as those from the South Asian nations.[3] China is acknowledged internationally as a leading contributor of "personnel to UN peacekeeping operations, providing more troops, police and observers than any other permanent member of the UN Security Council."[4] China has altogether sent more than ten thousand peacekeeping personnel on twenty-four UN peacekeeping missions, including the more than 2,100 currently deployed. Peacekeeping is a new form of China's aid to the needy.[5] China is currently adjusting its aid policies.[6]

China strictly defines peacekeeping as applicable only to UN or UN-related peacekeeping. There is currently no Chinese consideration of participating in non-UN or non-UN-related peacekeeping.[7]

> UN peacekeeping operations should comply with the UN Charter and all the basic principles that are proven effective, including neutrality, consent of parties concerned and nonuse of force except for self-defense, etc. China supports the enhancement of the UN's peacekeeping capacity and welcomes the Secretary-General's proposal on the establishment of strategic reserves and civilian police standby capacity. . . . Resources should be consolidated and limits of capacity respected and potential of the existing mechanisms fully tapped. The limited UN resources on peacekeeping should be rationally and effectively utilized.[8]

This paper will address lessons learned from China's experience with peacekeeping to date, constraints on China's future efforts of this type, the role of regional organizations, and governance in such operations. It will conclude with some discussion of both Chinese potential leadership and the scope for future China-U.S. peacekeeping cooperation.

Background

A number of factors readily explain Beijing's support of UN peacekeeping operations. First and foremost, today's China is no longer a critic of the existing international system but a more positive and conscious participant in it, in order to develop itself economically.[9] The possibility of a Chinese challenge to U.S. dominance, discussed widely in Western discourse, has been ruled out by Chinese decision makers. Second, China needs to act to make a contribution to the international community. Participation in peacekeeping is seen as a way of strengthening China's international contribution. "After receiving benefits from the international system, we have obligations to contribute to the international community and international system."[10]

These Chinese armored personnel carriers, operated by Chinese "blue helmet" peacekeeping soldiers, were deployed to Sudan. They are illustrative of the new capabilities, and also the high level of professionalism that Chinese peacekeepers bring to any mission. Beijing has also recently set up the most advanced training facilities for UN peacekeeping troops in the world.

Third, international peacekeeping, well supported by the Chinese public, is making a contribution consistent with Chinese capabilities (力所能及). However, some Chinese commentators have suggested a revised principle—that China can do more, in order to undertake more responsibilities (更大责任). Fourth, the continuation of China's export-led and resources-driven economic-growth model makes for the emergence of a hot debate on China's "overseas interests" and "the protection of such interests" (海外利益保护). A conflict-stricken world, particularly as regions of Africa, is a threat to China's increasing overseas interests.[11]

Fifth, Hu Jintao has recently called for ethical principles to play a larger role in Chinese foreign policy, which has previously emphasized only economic development. He underscored the need for China's foreign policy to reflect China's "moral appeal" (道义感召力).[12] Sixth, UN peacekeeping is consistent with Beijing's overall embrace of multilateralism, though China does not always welcome multilateral approaches—for example, concerning the South China Sea dispute. Finally, international peacekeeping has developed in China as part of the overall effort to modernize the armed forces. As part of this wider effort, China should build up a world-class navy like other established big powers, or at least like other rising powers, such as India. But it is still worth noting that China's Ministry of Defense recently replied to a question of China's overseas military base by stating that China has no plan to build up overseas military bases.[13] However, the debate is mainly not about whether or not the Chinese military should be modernized or "revolutionized" but about how China uses its new military forces. The political leaders have made clear that China needs to "strengthen all aspects of the army," to make it better able to win "informationized local wars" and respond to "multiple security threats."[14] China repeatedly tells the world that its strengthened military will contribute to world peace by multilateralizing itself. For example, "a naval force with advanced armaments and enhanced capabilities will contribute more to UN-led antiterrorism, antipiracy and disaster-relief missions."[15]

China's foreign-policy doctrine is a combination of the continuation of the "low key" foreign policy and the new exploration of adaptation to a changed world. In this respect, the increase of China's international responsibility is a key issue. At this point, the issue has been much debated internally within China without reaching a clear conclusion.

Lessons from China's Experience with International Peacekeeping

Lesson 1: International learning is not an easy or short process. China has learned a lot about how to coordinate constructively and harmonize the national interest and the international interest. In the UN, because of the existence of complex big-power politics, China has had to battle for its narrowly defined national concerns, such as the Taiwan issue, which has affected China's voting behavior. For example, in 1999, due to Taiwan's "established diplomatic ties with Macedonia," China vetoed the renewal of a mandate for the United Nations peacekeeping force in the Former Yugoslav Republic. China had no other option but to use the veto power for safeguarding its sovereignty rights. In recent years, as China's engagement with peacekeeping has deepened, China no longer simply uses the veto power at the Security Council. To some degree, overconcentration on China's own concerns had lowered China's role in representing the interests of the international community in general and the developing world in particular.[16] A more progressive and pragmatic view has developed, allowing China to participate meaningfully, for example, in the UN peacekeeping mission recently in Haiti, which had no diplomatic relations with Beijing.

Lesson 2: International peacekeeping is both politically sensitive and logistically difficult. In deciding on peacekeeping missions and their inputs, politically, China has to be cautious. Logistically, China has to assess the effectiveness of the mission in saving lives and resources. China has noticed that its peacekeeping missions may be easily interpreted by some parties in civil wars as a neo-imperialist intervention by a non-Western, rising power.[17]

Lesson 3: China has long concentrated on "easy" parts of the UN peacekeeping missions, but this policy is being reexamined. Focusing on clear issues, such as humanitarian relief, has allowed Beijing to avoid intrusion into sensitive sovereignty issues that sometimes generate violent conflict. Now, China is being pressed to take part in more difficult parts of the mission but is not fully ready to do so.[18] Still, China's nonintervention principle is now being revisited and revised.[19] Nevertheless, Beijing is always too cautious. China refuses to be a well prepared and equipped international leader in peacekeeping. Deng Xiaoping's "not-take-lead" (不带头) dictum is still valid in China's efforts in supporting peacekeeping.

Lesson 4: There is little evidence to suggest that China will take the initiative to reform UN peacekeeping. International scholars have called for the emergence of new concepts, doctrines, rules, and theories of peacekeeping. Of course, they argue wishfully that such things must be "with Chinese characteristics."[20] China should adopt and internalize common international theories and practices of peacekeeping, as the practice of peacekeeping is far from perfect; China should develop new approaches and strategies to contribute to it.

Lesson 5: China is still mainly practicing the principles and norms of "first generation" peacekeeping. These norms include consent of the parties, neutrality, nonuse of force, and unarmed peacekeeping. The ideas help maintain a peacekeeping consensus with the developing world, but China's reluctance to embrace more advanced peacekeeping paradigms, such as peace-enforcing and the "responsibility to protect," creates a principled gap with other state players of peace missions, especially the West, in the evolution of peacekeeping.

Lesson 6: China's engagement with non-UN peacekeeping is relatively weak and limited. China has not joined any non-UN peacekeeping operations, operated by such multilateral military and political organizations as NATO. The Global Peace Operations Initiative (GPOI), sponsored by the United States in 2004, is an example of a non-UN program.[21] Possibly, in the future, a number of regional organizations, such as the Shanghai Cooperation Organization (SCO) and ASEAN, may operate such programs. China should broaden and deepen its peacekeeping engagement to include non-UN peacekeeping operations.

Constraints on Chinese Peacekeeping

China's engagement with peacekeeping perhaps helps internationalize its military and police. In other words, China's military and police, which had generally not undertaken external operations since the end of the Cold War, have now broadened their worldviews to familiarize themselves further, from an institutional standpoint, with this relatively new area of international security and have accumulated needed international experience to standardize the Chinese force.

As a truly developing country with huge domestic imperatives, problems, and vulnerabilities, China must still undertake only limited responsibilities—surely and inevitably, in terms of its ability to deliver international public goods. But if China decides to sustain its role in peacekeeping, financial limits should not be an unresolvable problem. The real limits to growth of China's peacekeeping efforts are mainly not financial but political.

The sovereignty principle clearly decides the limit of China's peacekeeping depth. Today, Chinese leaders realize that most peacekeeping activities are essentially international interventions into domestic conditions. Thus, China is liberating itself from such doctrinal constraints, seeking a more flexible or revised attitude regarding sovereignty and nonintervention. Actually, China now pursues a conditional and constructive intervention to some degree, in various cases.[22]

The gap between China and the Western countries over a key norm—"responsibility to protect" (R2P)—as the alternative to nonintervention in peacekeeping has narrowed. But to China the norm is still questionable. At least, there are implicit or explicit differences between China and the West over interpretation. The report of the International Commission on Intervention and State Sovereignty (2001) delivered the principle, and initially China disagreed and even opposed it. Later on, China's attitude to the norm significantly changed, which once again showed that China's general attitude toward peacekeeping continues to evolve. China echoed the international community in declaring, "No reckless intervention should be allowed. When a massive humanitarian crisis occurs, it is the legitimate concern of the international community to ease and defuse the crisis. Any response to such a crisis should strictly conform to the UN Charter and the opinions of the country and the regional organization concerned should be respected. It falls on the Security Council to make the decision in the framework of the UN in light of specific circumstances that should lead to a peaceful solution as far as possible. Wherever it involves enforcement actions, there should be more prudence in the consideration of each case." China worries that overemphasis of R2P and the use of force cannot fundamentally solve the various domestic conflicts.[23]

In some places (Congo, Sudan/Darfur, and other African spots in particular) that are geostrategically crucial, controversial, and complicated, China's peacekeeping role has become more difficult. China has to consider the geopolitical and diplomatic costs of such peacekeeping operations. China needs to be more effective in its political communications and public diplomacy to convince the host country and international stakeholders to be free of any strategic concern or doubt as to China's motivation in peacekeeping participation. A key question is: Do the United States and other traditional peacekeeping powers welcome China's expanding and leading role in peacekeeping? For this, China needs to increase its mutual trust and confidence building with others.

Regional Organizations

China's role in UN peacekeeping is increasingly evolving through the frameworks of regional organizations. China hopes that regional organizations will play a larger role in peacekeeping. An apparent advantage for China is its familiarity with troubled regions and their regional organizations. China realizes that one of the fundamental contemporary trends of the world now is *regionalization*. So, China has gradually developed its system of regional policies, including China's European Union (EU) policy, its Africa policy, and its Asia policy as newly identified and added important dimensions of China's foreign policy. China has been keeping good relations with regional organizations in the developing world, such as the African Union (or AU, which has great political will to play in its own regional peacekeeping but lacks capacity) and recently ASEAN, not to mention the SCO, which is a major stakeholder in the stability and reconstruction of Afghanistan. An inclusive international/UN peacekeeping solution to finish the U.S. and NATO missions in Afghanistan may actually be a good arrangement for future development. Therefore, friendliness and other advantages (e.g., proximity) make China's peacekeeping role in such regions relatively easier.

China has encouraged UN-AU enhanced cooperation for delivering effective support for Africa in the field of peacekeeping activities: "Currently, about 75 percent of the UN peacekeepers are deployed in Africa, and about 70 percent of the UN peacekeeping assessed contributions are spent in Africa. The African Union is playing an ever important role in preventing and resolving the conflicts in Africa. The United Nations should continue to strengthen its partnership with the African Union in the area of peacekeeping operations and help Africa improve its capacity-building for peacekeeping operations."[24]

On the Darfur issue, China proposed and supported a joint operation between the United Nations and the African Union. As an outcome, through China's mediation, the African Union/UN Hybrid Operation in Darfur (UNAMID) was created. In the 2009 Forum on China and Africa Cooperation (FOCAC) at Sharm al-Sheikh, Egypt, China further committed itself to provide assistance and enhance cooperation with the UN and AU in the prevention, management, and resolution of regional conflicts in Africa. China promised to contribute to UN peacekeeping missions in Africa, strengthen cooperation with countries concerned in the UN Peacebuilding Commission, and support countries in their postwar reconstruction processes, as well as to deepen cooperation with African countries in peacekeeping training and exchanges and in the further building of peacekeeping capacity in Africa.[25]

The SCO also could play a role in future peacekeeping missions. The organization does not mention the term "peacekeeping" in its communiqués, declarations, or statements, but one Chinese scholar, Zheng Hao, a former visiting fellow at the Brookings

Institution, has proposed that the SCO take up a peacekeeping role in Afghanistan's postwar and post-NATO reconstruction process.[26]

According to its newly approved charter, ASEAN is the only regional/subregional security community (the so-called ASEAN Security Community) in Asia. In 2004, Indonesia has proposed the formation of a Southeast Asian peacekeeping force that could one day help settle disputes like those in Aceh and the southern Philippines. The UN has welcomed the proposal.[27] Such a peacekeeping force, however, may be unlikely, as within ASEAN it remains difficult to reach consensus. ASEAN's "internal" security coordination is a precondition to any role played by a non-ASEAN member, such as China, in regional peacekeeping. If there is no ASEAN invitation, China is unlikely to send peacekeeping troops to the subregion.

Local Governance

By peacekeeping, China plays a unique governance role—strengthening local capacities after a conflict or war. China's role in rebuilding postconflict countries has already illustrated one of its potential roles in international peacekeeping, helping improve local governance.

The UN emphasizes "complex peacekeeping operations," a number of postconflict peace-building and domestic reconstruction processes—confidence-building measures, power-sharing arrangements, electoral support, strengthening of the rule of law, human rights protection, economic and social development, and the building up of infrastructure—as more important than traditional, simple peacekeeping. China's membership in a new UN body, the Peacebuilding Commission, shows that it also endorses peace building and its institutionalization.[28]

China's role in Afghanistan can be viewed from the local-governance perspective. There is no Chinese peacekeeping presence in Afghanistan. However, there has been an interesting Chinese internal debate (triggered by NATO's exploration of cooperation with China for stabilizing Afghanistan) on whether or not to contribute peacekeeping forces there. In the foreseeable future, China will not send such troops. Nevertheless, China is involved in Afghanistan. China attended all Afghanistan-related international conferences, including the Kabul International Conference in July 2010, which was the first such meeting held on the Afghan soil. As a neighbor of Afghanistan, China is a major donor, providing development assistance to Afghanistan's reconstruction. According to the Chinese foreign minister, China provided a total of more than nine hundred million renminbi of grant assistance and canceled $19.5 million of Afghanistan's mature debts between 2002 and 2009. We have built seven projects for Afghanistan, including the Jomhuri Hospital (Republican Hospital), rehabilitated the Parwan irrigation project, provided fifteen batches of assistance materials, trained 781 Afghans from various professions, and received ninety-four Afghan students through government scholarships. In March 2010, China announced that it would provide another 160 million yuan of grant assistance to Afghanistan, to be used on infrastructure, medical care, health, and education programs.

China has increased the scale of personnel training for Afghanistan. In 2010, China trained over two hundred Afghan officials and technical personnel. During 2011, China increased the number of government scholarships to Afghanistan from thirty every year to fifty. This will bring the total number of Afghan students studying in China on various scholarships to around a hundred. China overcomes difficulties and continues to build assistance projects in Afghanistan that benefit the local communities. The presidential multifunction center built by China has been completed, and work has started on its auxiliary projects. We will build a national technology, science, and education center for Afghanistan and a teaching building and a guesthouse for Kabul University. China has given Afghanistan preferential tariff treatment to support its economic development. In 2009, Beijing and Kabul exchanged letters on zero-tariff treatment for certain Afghan exports to China, more than four thousand items.[29]

Traditionally, peacekeeping is predominantly done by "hard power"—military and police peacekeepers. Today, peacekeeping includes more soft dimensions of power, in local political, economic, and social governance processes. Providing effective development assistance to countries like Afghanistan should be seen as an innovative aspect of peace missions.

Leadership for China in Peacekeeping

Leadership undertaken by either established powers (especially the United States) or emerging powers (especially China) is key to secure the success of global governance and peace. Gill and Huang observe, "Chinese peacekeepers are consistently rated among the most professional, well-trained, effective and disciplined contingents in UN peacekeeping Operations"; "Chinese personnel are increasingly involved in mission leadership and decision making"; and that "China's high profile in peacekeeping reinforces both the perceived legitimacy and the effectiveness of UN peace missions."[30] Considering China's position in the UN and in the conflict-stricken world, these Chinese achievements and its performance may lead to a much-needed international peacekeeping leadership—Chinese leadership.

So far, China has refused to adopt boldly a leadership position in peacekeeping. But China has repeatedly declared that it is a "responsible great power" (负责任大国). I predict that China will be a special leader in international peacekeeping. Peacekeeping leadership does not contradict China's overall low-key foreign policy but rather helps ease tension between a rising China and the others, as peacekeeping participation is a "soft" use of China's growing power. Also, peacekeeping leadership helps strengthen Chinese-Western mutually complementary cooperation. Regarding personnel, for example, the shortage of qualified and available peacekeepers is always a common problem, but China can supply many more than can others.

On China's general role in the world, the West sends contradictory signals. The West asks for, presses for, and encourages China's bigger role, and China promises such a role.[31] But China's leadership or potential is easily perceived, judged, and misunderstood as a challenge to the Western liberal order. Questions arise: As China explores new ideas for the reform of international peacekeeping, would this lead to Chinese-Western mutual accommodation or greater suspicion? If China plays a future role as a peacekeeping leader, will the West fully accept that role and not be afflicted by the fading of its own traditional leadership?

China-U.S. Cooperation

The second Chinese-American joint statement by Presidents Hu Jintao and Barack Obama, issued on 17 November 2009 in Beijing, reported, "The two sides also discussed the importance of UN peacekeeping operations in promoting international peace and security."[32] This is a positive and hopeful development, because peacekeeping enriches and redirects China-U.S. relations. What is the Chinese-American common ground with respect to peacekeeping? How can the two states cooperate under the framework of UN peacekeeping?

U.S. airborne troops patrol together with Chinese People's Armed Police in Haiti during January 2010 after the devastating earthquake. While unusual at this point, the two militaries should expand this form of cooperation in order to meet extensive nontraditional security challenges in the twenty-first century.

On 29 January 2010, Chinese media, including the official Xinhua News Agency, prominently covered a rare moment: "China, US Peacekeepers Conduct Joint Patrol in Haiti."[33] This may be an early harbinger of Sino-American cooperation in this regard.

On 19 January China and the United States issued the new joint statement during President Hu Jintao's state visit to Washington. The statement focused on a specific peacekeeping issue—the independence of South Sudan: "Regarding Sudan, the United States and China agreed to fully support the North-South peace process, including full and effective implementation of Sudan's Comprehensive Peace Agreement. The two sides stressed the need for all sides to respect the result of a free, fair, and transparent referendum. Both the United States and China expressed concern on the Darfur issue. . . . Both the United States and China have a continuing interest in the maintenance of peace and stability in the wider region."[34]

Peacekeeping may play a positive role in facilitating "cooperative, comprehensive and positive China-U.S. ties." Given the current difficulties of China-U.S. military-to-military exchanges, the two sides can reach consensus to see peacekeeping as a relatively easier and softer area that can foster deepened China-U.S. security cooperation. There are still obstacles that could slow down China-U.S. military-to-military exchanges, but the conduct of peacekeeping cooperation can help promote these exchanges.

The ongoing reform of UN peacekeeping operations is a good opportunity to forge Chinese-American joint leadership in order to realize the ideal of *Charting a New Horizon for UN Peacekeeping*.[35] For this, China and the United States can cosponsor programs, including international conferences on the reform of UN peacekeeping practices.

China and the United States may continue to diverge over some principles and paradigms of peacekeeping, but the differences should not be exaggerated. Chinese scholars think peacekeeping is a form of protecting and improving universal human rights. China's embrace of humanitarianism in the form of multilateral peacekeeping and peace building should also be helpful in narrowing China-U.S. differences over human rights.[36] A good start on bilateral peacekeeping cooperation would be joint sponsorship of a peacekeeping training program.

In his first visit to Afghanistan, on 28 March 2010, President Obama said, "Our strategy includes a military effort that takes the fight to the Taliban while creating the conditions for greater security and a transition to the Afghans; but also a civilian effort that improves the daily lives of the Afghan people."[37] China will not send its troops or open its border for assisting the military mission in Afghanistan, but it plays a civilian-governance role in the strengthening local economic and social development. The United States should affirm China's special contribution as Afghanistan's neighbor.

So actually there is already tacit, yet important Chinese-American cooperation on the difficult Afghanistan issue.

Conclusion

China has learned many lessons from its participation in peacekeeping. It has become a major "responsible stakeholder" in the transformation of international peacekeeping. In the future, with the overcoming of constraints on and difficulties in undertaking more international responsibilities, peacekeeping will be a continuously dynamic sector in helping further develop China's relations with the international community.

Global peacekeeping currently lacks global leadership. China is exploring a proper leadership role as a new form of contribution commensurate with its new power and consequent moral obligations. But the nation still conducts a cautious, or careful, foreign policy, in order to not be misunderstood strategically as a challenge to American world leadership. A better China-U.S. division of labor—coleadership in peacekeeping—is crucial not only to strengthen China-U.S. military cooperation but to transform further the current practice of peacekeeping.

Notes

1. Su Yincheng, "中国'蓝盔'享誉世界" [Chinese "Blue Berets" Have Won Praise from the World], *People's Daily*, 2 April 2010, p. 20.

2. Wang Yizhou, "中国维和应'创造性介入,'" [China's Peacekeeping Should Constitute "Constructive Involvement"], 中国报道 [China Report], no. 2 (2010), p. 59.

3. Waheguru Pal Singh Sidhu, "Regional Groups and Alliances," in *The Oxford Handbook on the United Nations*, ed. Thomas G. Weiss and Sam Daws (New York: Oxford Univ. Press, 2007), p. 227.

4. Bates Gill and Chin-Hao Huang, *China's Expanding Role in Peacekeeping: Prospects and Policy Implications*, SIPRI Policy Paper 25 (Solna, Swed.: Stockholm International Peace Research Institute, November 2009).

5. Wang Yizhou, "China's Peacekeeping Should Constitute 'Constructive Involvement,'" p. 59.

6. Pang Zhongying, "China's Changing Foreign Aid Principle," 瞭望 [Outlook Weekly] (Beijing), 30 August 2010.

7. Wei Yanwei (Deputy Director of Peacekeeping Affairs, Ministry of Defense) (remarks at Peacekeeping International Symposium, Beijing, 29 November 2009), Xinhua.

8. People's Republic of China Ministry of Foreign Affairs, *China's Position Paper on UN Reforms* (Beijing: 8 June 2005).

9. 章百家 [Zhang Baijia] (Deputy Director, Communist Party of China [CPC] History Research, Central Committee of the CPC), "中国外交成长历程中的观念变迁：从革命的、民族的视角到发展的、全球的视野" [Ideational Change in Chinese Diplomacy: From the Revolutionary and Nationalist to the Evolutionary and Global], 外交评论 [Foreign Affairs Review], no. 3 (2009).

10. 马小军 [Ma Xiaojun] (Central Party School), "一个世界性大国的贡献与责任" [A World Power's Contribution and Responsibility], *China Report*, no. 2 (2010).

11. For example, Zhou Qi, "新维和观与中国国家利益" [New Peacekeeping Ideas and China's National Interest], 求索 [Explore], no. 3 (2005).

12. Hu Jintao spoke at the eleventh National Ambassadorial and Envoy Conference; see politics.people.com.cn/GB/1024/9687405.html.

13. Cui Xiaohuo, "Navy Has No Plan for Overseas Bases," *China Daily*, 11 March 2010.

14. Wen Jiabao, *Government Work Report to the National People's Congress* (Beijing: 5 March 2010).

15. Cui, "Navy Has No Plan for Overseas Bases."

16. 赵磊 [Zhao Lei], 建构和平: 中国对联合国外交行为的演进 [Constructing Peace: Evolution of China Diplomatic Behavior toward the United Nations] (Beijing: Jiuzhou Press, 2011), p. 234.
17. Wang Yizhou, "China's Peacekeeping Should Constitute 'Constructive Involvement,'" p. 59.
18. Zhao Lei, *Constructing Peace,* p. 218.
19. Pang Zhongying, "China's Nonintervention Question," *Journal of Global Responsibility to Protect* 1, no. 2 (March 2009).
20. Wang Yizhou, "China's Peacekeeping Should 'Constructive Involvement,'" p. 59.
21. On GPOI, see Gill and Huang, *China's Expanding Role in Peacekeeping,* pp. 22–23.
22. See Pang, "China's Nonintervention Question."
23. Pang Sen, 联合国维和中国在行动 [In UN Peacekeeping, China Is in Action], *China Report,* no. 2 (2010), p. 45.
24. Ambassador Liu Zhenmin (statement at "Open Debate of the Security Council on UN Peacekeeping Operations," New York, 5 August 2009).
25. *Declaration of the Sharm-el-Sheikh Forum on China-Africa Cooperation (FOCAC),* Fourth Ministerial FOCAC Conference (Sharm al-Sheikh, Egypt: 9 November 2009), available at www.focac.org/.
26. Zheng Hao, *The Shanghai Cooperation Organization and NATO: Possible Collaboration on Afghanistan Reconstruction* (New York: Brookings Institution, 2009).
27. "Indonesia Proposes Southeast Asian Peacekeeping Force," *Association of Southeast Asian Nations,* 21 February 2004, www.aseansec.org/.
28. People's Republic of China Ministry of Foreign Affairs, *China's Position Paper on UN Reforms.*
29. "Remarks by H. E. Yang Jiechi, Minister of Foreign Affairs of the People's Republic of China, at the Kabul International Conference on Afghanistan," 20 July 2010.
30. Gill and Huang, *China's Expanding Role in Peacekeeping.*
31. Peter Mandelson, "We Want China to Lead," *New York Times,* 11 February 2010.
32. White House, Office of the Press Secretary, "U.S.-China Joint Statement: Beijing, China," 17 November 2009, available at www.whitehouse.gov/.
33. "China, US Peacekeepers Conduct Joint Patrol in Haiti," *China Daily,* 29 January 2010.
34. White House, Office of the Press Secretary, "U.S.-China Joint Statement," 19 January 2011, available at www.whitehouse.gov/.
35. United Nations, *A New Partnership Agenda: Charting a New Horizon for UN Peacekeeping* (New York: Dept. of Peacekeeping Operations and Dept. of Field Support, July 2009), available at www.un.org/.
36. Dr. Yuan Zhengqing (remarks at Conference on Global Challenges and Global Governance, Beijing, 17 March 2010).
37. White House, Office of the Press Secretary, "Remarks by the President to the Troops: Clamshell, Bagram Airfield," 28 March 2010, available at www.whitehouse.gov/.

Chinese Peacekeeping in the Asia-Pacific

A Case Study of East Timor

Lyle J. Goldstein and Kathleen A. Walsh

Numerous surveys have appeared in recent years on China's growing role in United Nations (UN) peacekeeping operations. These analyses provide valuable insights into China's changing foreign- and security-policy decision making and cite myriad reasons that might underlie Beijing's new approach to UN peacekeeping. Some more recent analyses have begun to look more specifically at China's role in select UN missions in order to provide greater fidelity in understanding Beijing's evolving role in NTS operations. This analysis follows the latter approach, by examining specifically China's role and interests in the series of UN missions to East Timor since 2000. It seeks to identify the rationales cited for China's continued engagement in this unprecedented UN peacekeeping mission as well as the implications for future Chinese participation in such operations.

The UN's peacekeeping efforts in East Timor, now the independent state of Timor-Leste, date back more than a decade (see the table). After centuries as a Portuguese colony, followed by decades of Indonesian occupation, the East Timorese were given an opportunity in 1999 by the Indonesian leadership to decide via referendum whether to become an autonomous region remaining under Indonesian rule or an independent state. The first UN Mission in East Timor (UNAMET) deployed for the purpose of supporting this referendum process. However, following the vote, which was by a large majority in favor of independence, widespread militia-led violence broke out and threatened further chaos, raising the specter of a new failed state. To prevent this and help restore order, the International Force for East Timor (INTERFET) mission, led by neighboring Australia, deployed shortly after the vote and quickly restored stability. A new UN Transitional Administration in East Timor (UNTAET) mission took temporary sovereignty over East Timor, with Timorese concurrence, in order to help rebuild the state and ready it for independence, which came in 2002.

The latter mission, authorized by Chapter VII of the UN Charter, would be one of only a handful of recent UN missions charged with taking over temporary sovereignty of a nation-state in order to restore it to full functionality. Subsequent UN missions have furthered these efforts to establish a well-functioning, sovereign, independent state of Timor-Leste while weathering a series of interim security and stability setbacks. Insurgent uprisings in 2006 and subsequent clashes led Australia—at the behest of the government of Timor-Leste (GoTL)—to head up an International Stabilization Force (ISF) to reestablish order and stability, especially following the assassination attempts in 2008 on the president and prime minister. China has been part of the UN Security Council–sanctioned efforts from almost the beginning of this story. But why would China seek to become involved in such a complex, long-term, and unprecedented peacekeeping operation? Moreover, what does China's participation in this particular series of peacekeeping missions suggest about contemporary Chinese foreign policy more generally?

Major Themes in PRC Peacekeeping Activities in East Timor / Timor-Leste

Chinese peacekeeping forces have been involved in East Timor / Timor-Leste operations since the start of the Transitional Administration in 1999. Though not sending military combat forces to the region, Beijing has deployed continuous detachments of UN civilian police (CIVPOL), including armed riot police, as well as military observers and liaison officers, along with several administrative staff personnel.

In evaluating both English- and Chinese-language sources, a number of common themes stand out, with distinct nuances evident in the latter, that could provide a deeper

Chinese Participation in UN Missions in East Timor / Timor-Leste
Source: United Nations, *Government of Australia*, SIPRI.
Notes:
a. Non-UN missions: INTERFET and ISF.
b. Political mission—UNOTIL (UN Office in East Timor); 2010 PRC contributions to UNMIT (UN Integrated Mission in Timor-Leste), 22 civilian police; 2 military observers (MILPER).

Mission	Years	Type	PRC Participation
UNAMET	Jun.–Oct. '99	Peacemaking	n/a
INTERFET[a]	Aug. '99–Feb. '00	Peace enforcement (non-UN)	n/a
UNTAET	Oct. '99–May '02	Peacekeeping	CIVPOL
		Peace enforcement	ADMIN
		Peace building	
UNMISET	May '02–May '05	Peace building	CIVPOL
UNOTIL[b]	May '05–Aug. '06	Peacekeeping	CIVPOL
		Peace building	
ISF[a]	May '06–present	Peace enforcement (supports UN)	n/a
UNMIT[b]	Aug. '06–Feb. '12	Peace building	CIVPOL
			MILPER

understanding of Beijing's approach in this case. The following is an overview of four overarching arguments cited for China's extensive involvement in the United Nations' long-term peacekeeping efforts in East Timor.

Theme 1: A Changing International and Regional Security Environment

A common theme found in studies examining China's enhanced post–Cold War participation in UN peacekeeping operations is change in the international and regional security environments. A 2009 Swedish Defence Research Agency (SDRA) survey of major studies on Chinese peacekeeping activities identified the following as commonly cited key security- and foreign policy–oriented rationales for growing PRC involvement in UN peacekeeping operations:[1]

- Shared security interests with the rest of the world
- China's rising comfort level in the peacekeeping regime
- Changes in Beijing's foreign and security policy
- Beijing's concerns about its international reputation
- Efforts to counterbalance perceived U.S. hegemony, while keeping a low profile
- China's drive to isolate Taipei diplomatically
- Prevention of security threats from failing states.

After thirteen Chinese sailors were killed in a criminal attack along the Mekong River in October 2011, Beijing quickly responded by creating a small task force of lightly armed river vessels operated by the Ministry of Public Security to patrol the volatile upper sections of the river in cooperation with neighbors including Laos, Myanmar, and Thailand. This is an important example of the new focus on nontraditional security issues in Chinese foreign policy.

As this general list suggests, China's growing acceptance of UN peacekeeping activities was in part likely a function of new opportunities due to China's rising international power and stature, as well as of newly arising challenges, such as failed states and terrorist enclaves, that threatened Beijing's changing, more comprehensive national-security interests. In the specific case of East Timor, China's decision to take a more active approach and support the initial UNTAET mission might also conceivably have been tied to a series of extraneous events with national- and regional-security repercussions for China. These included the aftermath of the 1997 Asian financial crisis, the then-still-strained status of U.S.-China relations, and the accidental bombing in 1999 by American aircraft of China's mission in Belgrade, as part of a NATO-authorized (as opposed to UN-authorized) military intervention.[2] It is as yet unclear whether or how any or all of these events might have impacted decisions made in Beijing to intercede in East Timor as part of the UNTAET mission, but both English- and Chinese-language studies of Chinese peacekeeping decisions suggest a change in strategy or policy due in part to changes in the security environment.

Notably, for instance, both English- and Chinese-language sources emphasize the 1999 period and the Timor mission as collectively being a critical turning point in Chinese policy making vis-à-vis participation in UN peacekeeping. As Chinese scholar He Yin notes, "1999 marked the beginning of a new era for China's active participation in UNPKO [UN peacekeeping operations]. . . . China for the first time signaled that an UNPKO with an enforcement-featured mandate like that of UNTAET could be politically acceptable." Chinese-language sources highlight similar strategic interests. For instance, a 2007 analysis by Niu Zhongjun states, "Because of the complexity of the East Timor questions, our participation in the UN peacekeeping operations in East Timor . . . should be viewed as a major foreign policy decision, illustrating China's disposition to use the UN as the main tool to cope with international conflicts."[3] Niu goes on to say, "Although China dispatched civilian observers for the first time ever to participate in the peacekeeping activities to support the UN's transitional authority in East Timor, actually the scale was not so small, so that up to this point the personnel involved are up to two hundred. . . . This deed illustrates China acting as a responsible great power, and thus China received universal praise in the international community."[4]

Also considered in Chinese-language articles and after-action lessons-learned analyses, however, are the mission parameters, which at first appeared to be relatively straightforward but ultimately proved quite complex. Nonetheless, China's participation continues and appears to be viewed as a success, by both PRC and UN authorities. A volume reviewing Chinese lessons learned highlights several key parameters—"cooperation of the Indonesia government"; "a relatively benign security environment . . . [where] there are relatively few guns, and land mines are not major problem"; "vigorous support of the international community"; and "the clear-cut nature of the aid activities"—as critical to consideration of PRC participation in the East Timor operations.[5]

Also according to Chinese-language sources, China's regional security interests formed a key factor in deciding to become engaged in Timorese peacekeeping, as highlighted in the following:

- "East Timor is a small country that is quite a distance from our country, but considered from the perspective of our foreign policy, it occupies a position that cannot be ignored."[6]
- "East Timor . . . is located proximate to where sea transport lines pass from the Indian Ocean through the Torres Strait to the Pacific Ocean, a strategically important position."[7]
- "Developing friendly relations with East Timor from the earliest possible point is also beneficial to consolidating the momentum for China-ASEAN relations."[8]
- "Regarding military affairs, in July 2002 the Defense Minister of East Timor . . . visited China, suggesting a new high level of importance to the PRC–East Timor relationship."[9]

Not surprisingly (although it is not emphasized as prominently in English-language analyses), Beijing also appears to have taken PRC-Indonesian relations into account in deciding whether and how to be engaged in Timorese peacekeeping, being careful not to undermine long-term prospects for enhanced Sino-Indonesian relations. Niu Zhongjun's analysis of the Timor mission specifically notes an emphasis on building PRC-Indonesia/Timorese relations dating back to a 1990 visit by Li Peng, then premier, to resume relations with Indonesia (severed since 1967) and repeated visits by President Jiang Zemin in the late 1990s, including during the 1997 Asian financial crisis. Niu notes, "The East Timor peacekeeping issue not only did not block the development of Chinese-Indonesian relations, but on the contrary in large measure accelerated the rapprochement between the two countries. This stands as one of the major successes of Chinese foreign policy."[10] Moreover, according to Chinese-language assessments, shared history of ideological and cultural connections between the Indonesian, Timorese, and Chinese peoples appear to have served as an additional element of decision making.[11]

Theme 2: Changing International Peacekeeping Norms

The second rationale cited for China's expanding role in international peacekeeping, specifically in East Timor, is what appears to be a subtle change in China's long-standing foreign policy principles governing international interventions in an era of changing international peacekeeping norms. As noted in the SDRA survey, China's overseas activities have long been guided by the "principles of non-interference and sovereignty . . . and

China's opposition against the use of force."[12] Given this, the U.S. Department of Defense annual report for 2011 notes:

> Prior to 2002, Beijing generally avoided participation in UN peacekeeping operations (PKO), due to lingering skepticism of the international system and a long-stated policy of non-interference in other countries' internal affairs. China's participation from 1991–1993 in the UN Transitional Authority in Cambodia marked a notable exception to this policy. China's attitude towards UN PKOs has changed dramatically over the past decade, particularly since Hu Jintao promulgated the New Historic Missions in 2004.[13]

Indeed, most studies on Chinese peacekeeping highlight Beijing's growing flexibility on the need to protect Westphalian norms and principles as well as an apparent growing acceptance of more extensive UN authority over traditional state sovereignty when faced with overwhelming challenges to state power and regional stability. Yet it remains uncertain exactly how supportive Beijing is when it comes to condoning more extensive peace-building and peace-enforcement activities, in this or other UN peacekeeping missions. On the basis of discussions with PRC interlocutors, it is possible that thinking in Beijing might have even retreated from a more expansive, comprehensive view of UN peacekeeping. Yet the emphasis among English-language sources on such normative changes suggests a relatively passive acceptance by Beijing of more interventionist norms permitting UN peacekeepers to play roles traditionally reserved to state sovereigns. This perspective, however, notwithstanding possible recent changes in outlook, comes into question in the case of East Timor. According to some English- and Chinese-language sources, Beijing might in fact have taken a more *activist* approach in deciding to send peacekeepers to East Timor. An early article by Bates Gill and James Reilly, for example, raised the prospect that Kosovo, in which NATO intervened in 1999 just prior to the East Timor referendum, might have played a part in Chinese decision making, a notion reiterated even more strongly in a recent Chinese-language analysis hinting that Beijing's decision was influenced by an opportunity to develop a new norm, or form, of intervention.[14] According to the latter:

> The NATO air attack against the Yugoslav Federation was undertaken under the pretext of a humanitarian intervention, and this situation had obvious similarities with the East Timor issue. Therefore, the East Timor issue in East Asia could also have followed the same path as the problematic Kosovo intervention. This was the chief reason that our country has taken an active role in participating in the peacekeeping activities in East Timor.[15]

Whether and to what degree the Kosovo precedent had any influence on Beijing's decision making when it came to intervening in East Timor remain unclear. One Chinese interlocutor insists definitively that there was absolutely no connection whatsoever.[16] Yet this prospect raises a more fundamental question of whether East Timor represents a leap forward in China's peacekeeping-policy decision making, as suggested earlier, and thus is a precursor to China's future involvement, or was in fact an exception due to historical timing. Whether this case was an exception, a new norm for Beijing, or something in between, a greater understanding of Chinese decision making is necessary to understand fully China's current and future roles in UN peacekeeping efforts.

Theme 3: PRC Economic Interests

A third theme commonly cited among English- and Chinese-language analyses of Chinese peacekeeping involvement in East Timor is that of economic interests. These span a range from trade and investment regionally and globally to arms export opportunities, along with an emphasis on access to strategic resources, particularly oil and gas.

Western analyses tend to highlight the strategic-resources angle. For example, a recent article argues that "one of China's primary interests in East Timor is to gain access to the country's oil and gas reserves."[17] East Timor sits in an unquestionably strategic location, nestled northwest of Darwin, Australia, with sovereign access to valuable seabed and underground resources that are being sought after for joint development by numerous suitors, including Australia, China, South Korea, and Thailand.[18]

Articles in Chinese, however, tend to emphasize in addition East Timor's own economic development and its prospects for following the PRC's economic model toward greater long-term prosperity. One article notes that "the East Timor side is extremely hopeful to study and learn from China's development experience. . . . East Timor is one of the poorest countries and is one of the twenty most backward countries in the whole world. . . . The extreme economic poverty limits the development of bilateral economic and trade relations. In this situation, energy cooperation has become a potentially bright spot for bilateral economic and trade cooperation."[19]

This last reference again brings to mind the notion that China might be interested in Timor peacekeeping operations, at least in part, as a means of shaping norms in the region, in this case economic norms. This would accord with China's broader foreign-policy goals of encouraging an open-door, "peaceful development" model of economic development, as well as foreign trade and investments that do not impose value-laden (read liberal democracy–oriented) conditions, in the same way that Beijing pursues its domestic economic reforms, foreign commercial trade interests, and overseas development assistance. Such a strategic approach would well match China's articulated long-term national and regional security interests, as well as help secure greater access to overseas markets and resources. The prospect of future arms exports to the region, as recently demonstrated by the sale of two Shanghai-class patrol boats to the GoTL, serves to further China's economic interests and possibly broader regional economic and geostrategic access and influence.

Theme 4: Potential for PRC Military Training, Experience, and Exposure

Finally, as the SDRA survey highlights, most English-language studies of Chinese peacekeeping activities emphasize "opportunities for training of personnel and gaining international experience." Yet there appears little focus on this dimension in Chinese-language sources studied thus far. This does not mean that China could not benefit in these ways from involvement in East Timor peacekeeping operations, but military training opportunities are likely limited in this case, given that no Chinese military combat forces are involved. Any training and experience are likely to be limited in the near term to civilian (armed) policing capabilities.

China is reputed also to be interested in becoming the region's base for CIVPOL training. The experience gained in Timor-based UN peacekeeping operations is likely to aid that objective. China's Ministry of National Defense and Public Security Bureau have established peacekeeping training centers at which Timorese military officers, including three dozen Timorese sailors, among others, have received training.[20] Civil policing is an area in which Beijing is eager and able to enhance its contributions to UN peacekeeping and to expand regionally the use of its domestic training facilities, at a time when such support is in high demand by UN headquarters.

Beijing has made counterterrorism a national priority in recent years. During preparations for the Olympics in 2008 and for the World Expo in 2010, China sought counsel from abroad, including from the United States, to improve its counterterrorism capabilities.

Outside of formal UN peacekeeping channels, there also exists the potential for enhanced Chinese military training, experience, and exposure via interactions with other nations' military personnel involved in operations supported through bilateral or regional programs with the Timor-Leste government. The United States, for example, has supported the UN missions in Timor-Leste through a separate "U.S. Support Group East Timor," which, under American command and control, supports projects that are typically short-term and high-impact.[21] The 11th Marine Expeditionary Unit and a U.S. Navy Seabee detachment, for instance, both engaged in HA/DR activities with GoTL counterparts in 2009, among other bilateral or multilateral cooperative engagement efforts.[22] After a six-month rotated deployment, a permanent detachment of Seabees arrived in February 2009 with a mission of supporting the GoTL and the country's efforts to improve its infrastructure and military capabilities, and to pursue societal reforms. Other donor nations are providing similar forms of training and support.

China's reasons for engaging in the Timor UN peacekeeping missions are likely some combination of the four rationales outlined above. Taken together, they suggest that a strategically important rationale exists, even if not fully explicated in the sources examined specific to the Timor case. Chinese sources emphasize that the mission is China's second in the Asia-Pacific (the other being Cambodia in the 1990s) and that both are viewed as successful engagements of overseas Chinese activity. Peacekeeping activities are also listed among rationales for China's expanding maritime capabilities; also, China's bilateral assistance to Timor-Leste includes building a new presidential palace and a ministry of foreign affairs.[23] The extent to which the Timor mission has been viewed in Beijing as a strategic opportunity—particularly given the limited role played by the United States and other Western powers in this instance, with the exception of Australia, which undertook the lead peacekeeping role—is hard to determine but is likely to have influenced China's continued presence there.

Conclusion and Implications for Future Chinese Peacekeeping

On the basis of a preliminary assessment of Chinese peacekeeping in East Timor, four key conclusions and implications can be drawn. First, China's involvement in the Timor peacekeeping missions constitutes a turning point in Chinese security-policy decision making. China's involvement in this case in particular, an Asia-Pacific peacekeeping mission, constitutes only Beijing's second deployment of peacekeepers in the region. It is an ongoing and still-evolving mission, and one that coincided with the beginning of a major increase in Chinese peacekeeping deployments worldwide, as well as with China's first-ever deployment of civil police forces in a complex peacekeeping case, one that covers the full spectrum of peacekeeping operations in a Chapter VII mission (in which "all necessary means" are authorized and complex issues governing international interventions—sovereignty, postcolonialization, and self-determination—are involved). These factors all contribute to a consensus that East Timor represents a key turning point in Chinese policy making. But it should not necessarily be taken as a template for future Chinese peacekeeping involvement. Although Chinese personnel have been involved through Timorese operations in nearly the full spectrum of comprehensive peacekeeping activities (combat excepted), Chinese interlocutors caution that this might represent more the exception than the rule in terms of future Chinese peacekeeping policy and decision making. What seems likely, however, is that Beijing will appoint greater priority to—and possibly be more actively and comprehensively involved in—peacekeeping activities that arise in the Asia-Pacific region, which it sees as in its vital national and regional interests.

Second, the surveyed Western, English-language sources focus on China's role in East Timor peacekeeping operations as part of a macro trend accepting more comprehensive forms of UN peacekeeping risks overlooking regional, bilateral, or distinct national interests involved. Beijing's decision making in this particular case is difficult to discern a decade later and might even have changed in the interim, national, regional, and international security environments having all changed as well. It is not clear that Beijing fully accepts the new norm of more comprehensive peacekeeping missions (e.g., accepting the "responsibility to protect" mandate) or that China accepted this at the time of initial intervention in East Timor. More dialogue on this topic—in both historical and contemporary contexts—is needed.

Third, China's role in East Timor peacekeeping is clearly viewed in Beijing as a dramatic success; UN observers view it also as a positive contribution—in March 2011 the GoTL resumed authority over all policy operations from United Nations forces. Whether or not East Timor becomes a template for future Chinese peacekeeping involvement (as UN experts seem to presume or hope), it will remain a positive example of China's role in international peacekeeping. In any case, given China's size, interests, and the expectations of the rest of the world, China's role in UN peacekeeping is likely to grow, especially if new Asia-Pacific operations arise. Moreover, as China's role and influence in UN peacekeeping activities expand, especially in the Asia-Pacific region, such developments could serve to salve—or, alternatively, exacerbate—sensitivities across a spectrum of issues. As such, expanded peacekeeping in the region and beyond could be a high-risk but also high-reward option for Beijing.

Finally, China's expanded interests and activities in UN peacekeeping raise new possibilities for U.S.-PRC security cooperation in Southeast Asia and elsewhere.[24] Timor-Leste is a case in which the United States is also involved, though in a limited way and independent of formal UN mission authorities. Nonetheless, there remains the potential for cooperative engagement. Based on the overlap, limited thus far, of American and Chinese aid to the GoTL and the confluence of interests in enhancing stability and security in this Asia-Pacific location, the potential exists for more collaborative or cooperative multilateral and confidence-building engagements involving the U.S. and PRC militaries in support of a more stable and secure Timor-Leste and also broader Asia-Pacific region.

Notes

1. Jerker Hellstrom, *Blue Berets under the Red Flag: China in the UN Peacekeeping System*, FOI-R-2772-SE (Stockholm: Swedish Defence Research Agency / FOI, June 2009), p. 33.

2. The authors thank Oystein Tunsjo for suggesting this point.

3. 牛仲君 [Niu Zhongjun], 中国参与东帝汶维和的原因级立场分析 [China's Peacekeeping Operations in East Timor: History and Analysis], 外交评论 [Foreign Policy Debates] (April 2007), p. 48.

4. Ibid., p. 51.

5. 赵宁 [Zhao Ning], 当代国际维和行动 [Contemporary International Peacekeeping Operations] (Beijing: Military Friendship Press, 2006), p. 176.

6. 李开盛, 周琦 [Li Kaisheng and Zhou Qi], 中国与东帝汶关系的历史现状及前景 [The History, Status Quo and Prospect of the Relationship between East Timor and China], 东南亚纵横 [Around Southeast Asia] (February 2004), p. 61.

7. Zhao, *Contemporary International Peacekeeping Operations*, p. 171.

8. Li and Zhou, "The History, Status Quo and Prospect of the Relationship between East Timor and China," p. 64.

9. Ibid., p. 63.

10. Niu, "China's Peacekeeping Operations in East Timor," pp. 50–51.

11. Ibid., p. 48; Li and Zhou, "The History, Status Quo and Prospect of the Relationship between East Timor and China," p. 61.

12. Hellstrom, *Blue Berets under the Red Flag*, p. 33.

13. U.S. Defense Dept., *Annual Report to Congress: Military and Security Developments Involving the People's Republic of China* (Washington, D.C.: Office of the Secretary of Defense, 2011), p. 66.

14. The initial UNTAET mission also met Beijing's two main preconditions pertaining to intervention, based on considerations over sovereignty—namely, that the mission be UN-authorized and that it have the support of the then-sovereign authority, the Indonesian government. Bates Gill and James Reilly, "Sovereignty, Intervention, and Peacekeeping: The View from Beijing," *Survival* 42, no. 3 (Autumn 2000), pp. 41–59.

15. Niu, "China's Peacekeeping Operations in East Timor," p. 51.

16. Statement to the author by a retired Chinese military officer, March 2010.

17. Ian Storey, "China's Inroads into East Timor," *China Brief* 9, no. 6 (March 2009).

18. The Australian firm Woodside Petroleum Ltd. was recently turned down by the GoTL in a plan to develop a liquid-natural-gas project in the Timor Sea; James Paton, "Woodside's Plans for Sunrise Won't Be Approved, East Timor Says," *Bloomberg Businessweek,* 12 April 2010. The Certain Maritime Arrangements in the Timor Sea (CMATS) Treaty between Timor Leste and Australia came into force in February 2007. Precise delimitation of seabed boundaries has been put off for future consideration, as agreed by both parties.

19. Li and Zhou, "The History, Status Quo and Prospect of the Relationship between East Timor and China," pp. 64–65.

20. Courtney Richardson, "A Responsible Power? China and the UN Peacekeeping Regime," *International Peacekeeping* 18, no. 3 (June 2011), pp. 286–97; Maj. Steven M. Johnson, U.S. Army, "ODC Timor Leste," U.S. Pacific Command brief, 23 April 2010; State Council Information Office, *China's National Defense in 2010* (Beijing: March 2011).

21. The authors are grateful to Professor George Oliver of the U.S. Naval War College for sharing this information.

22. Johnson, "ODC Timor Leste."

23. Ibid.; U.S. Defense Dept., *Annual Report to Congress,* p. 18.

24. This possibility is also noted in the latest U.S. Defense Department annual report on China's military development. See U.S. Defense Dept., *Annual Report to Congress,* p. 55.

Lessons from Mumbai

Chinese Analysts Assess the Threat of Maritime Terrorism

Sun Kai and Guo Peiqing

How to mobilize traditional capabilities, including military forces, to respond to nontraditional challenges is of much concern to national leaders around the globe. As for China, top leaders, including President Hu Jintao, expressed this concern in the Seventeenth National Congress, underlining the imperative "to enhance the ability of the military to respond to various kinds of threats, and fulfill multiple and diverse tasks."[1] Top PLA officers, including senior Chinese admirals, have emphasized the nontraditional security threat.[2]

Terrorists pose a grave threat to contemporary global society, and the prevention of terrorist attacks is now one of the major fields for international cooperation. This has been true especially since the 9/11 attacks a decade ago. India is also a country suffering from frequent terrorist attacks in recent years, and this peaked with the 2008 Mumbai terrorist attacks, which resulted in 195 deaths and more than three hundred wounded.[3] This paper will endeavor to elaborate on Chinese analyses of that tragic event and on lessons for China in countering potential terrorist threats emanating from the sea.

Nightmare at a Glance: The 2008 Mumbai Terrorist Attacks

The 2008 Mumbai terrorist attacks, which drew worldwide condemnation, first began on 26 November. By the early morning of 28 November, Mumbai police and security forces had finally ended the carnage and secured all sites except for the Taj Hotel. An action by India's National Security Guard (NSG) on 29 November (Operation BLACK TORNADO) resulted in the death of the last remaining attackers at the Taj Hotel. It took three days for NSG commandos to overcome these terrorists.

The 2008 Mumbai terrorist attack was unique in several ways.

First, the terrorists came to Mumbai via a sea route, sailing from Karachi on a Pakistani cargo vessel. They first hijacked an Indian fishing boat and murdered all its crew except for the captain, then proceeded to Mumbai. They killed the captain as they neared their destination. Coming by sea had several advantages over coming by land, allowing the terrorists to avoid Indian security checkpoints at the frontier or at airports; sailing on an Indian vessel also enabled them to avoid arousing the suspicion of the Indian coast guard.

Second, the terrorists were well trained and highly organized. They seem to have known locations of targets even better than the responding government forces. They were working together as a unit, and they coordinated with each other using high-tech equipment. They used hand signals to communicate across loud and crowded spaces. Apparently they received instructions while conducting this attack. They were sufficiently disciplined to continue their attack over many hours.[4]

Third, these terrorist attacks were carefully planned. This assessment includes the targets chosen, which were all commercial centers with high densities of people; the time of the attacks, which was during the peak hour at night; and the strategy of the attack, which was to attack the terminal first.[5]

Chinese Analyses of the Mumbai Terrorist Attacks

Immediately after the Mumbai terrorist attacks, a number of Chinese media paid close attention, addressing the following issues.

Who Were the Killers, and Where Were They From?

According to most Chinese specialists, there was a very high probability that these terrorists came from within India. Li Wei, an expert on antiterrorist studies with the China Institute of Contemporary International Relations in Beijing, was among the analysts taking this view. Shen Dingli, a professor with the Center for American Studies at Fudan University, was interviewed by *PLA Daily* and said that the root cause for terrorism lay in the country's social contradictions and also its anti-Western sentiments.[6] According to Liu Bosong, in addition to religious strife within India the external source of the killers was Pakistan, and that was the first country accused by India's leaders, immediately after the attack.[7] Not all the early speculations by Chinese analysts proved correct; later there was unambiguous evidence showing that those terrorists had originated in Pakistan and were trained there.[8]

What Are the Implications of the Terrorist Attacks for the South Asian Peninsula?

The Mumbai terrorist attacks cast a grey shadow over the peace process in South Asia, and the prospect of an India-Pakistan war seemed very real.[9] The possibility of military conflict between India and Pakistan was a common theme among several Chinese commentators, especially when both sides were reinforcing troops at the border.[10]

China too apparently deployed more troops to the border after the terrorist attacks, especially given the prospect of a war between India and Pakistan. Some commentators perhaps overestimated China's influence in the prospect of war between India and

Pakistan. According to one commentator, only China, rather than the United States, United Kingdom, or Russia, could curb India's belligerence against Pakistan.[11] Another piece a month later reinforced this view, asserting that the only reason why there was no war between India and Pakistan after the terrorist attacks was pressure applied by China.[12]

What Lessons Can China Learn from the Mumbai Attacks?

Much more media coverage of Chinese experts' analysis of the Mumbai terrorist attacks focused on lessons China could draw from this horrific event.

Maintaining Stability in Xinjiang. As maintaining stability is the top priority of the Chinese government's agenda, how to maintain stability in China, especially in those "hot spot areas," is naturally of major concern. This was particularly true after the warning by the Iranian president that the Mumbai terrorist planners might plot an attack on China.[13] Such warnings drew much Chinese expert attention to the issue of stability in the Uighur/Muslim-dominated Xinjiang, which is proximate to both India and Pakistan. In the view of Li Wei, who thinks the terrorists forces were mainly from within India, because of its long-standing internal religious and social conflict, China should draw the lesson of carefully handling potential conflicts in regions like Xinjiang.[14]

Capacity Building in Intelligence Collection. Quality intelligence is essential to nip terrorist plots in the bud. There seems to have been a paucity of coordination between the central security agencies and the local police in Mumbai. Focusing on this problem, analysts in China are very much concerned with China's counterterrorism intelligence capacity, and there are calls for stronger coordination and capacity building. According to a paper published in the *Journal of the Railway Police College,* the key task for counterterrorism is intelligence collection. China should invest more human and financial resources to institutionalizing the efforts in intelligence collection; mobilize mass power and build a civil system to counter terrorism; promote international cooperation and the pooling of information needed to keep our counterintelligence database up-to-date; and improve the quality and method of analyzing this information.[15] Li Wei too comments that there should be a breakthrough in securing high-quality intelligence, because one of the main difficulties in counterterrorism is the lack of quality intelligence.[16]

More Intensive Coastal Surveillance. The terrorists reached Mumbai through the sea route, and the gap in India's coastal surveillance was highlighted in media coverage. The lack of coordination between the coast guard and the navy enlarged the gap and made the case worse.[17] The need for strong coastal surveillance is common for all countries with coastlines. China has a coastline of about eighteen thousand kilometers, and coastal surveillance is of prominent importance, especially in the light of the Mumbai terrorist attacks. The need for building a stronger coast guard and better coordination between

China's massive ports are the most crucial nodes of Beijing's burgeoning economy. Safety and security in and around these trading hubs have evolved into a significant national priority.

the Chinese navy and various national coast guard elements predated the Mumbai attacks.

Stronger Counterterrorism Force Building. The Mumbai terrorist attacks also exposed how ill trained and equipped the local police were. Many police officers remained passive, because the terrorists outgunned them; the terrorists were better equipped, with modern and sophisticated weapons. Nor did Indian security forces have a well-designed rescue plan. Xu Hao, with the Public Security Bureau of Shanghai, writes that China should learn from the Mumbai terrorist attacks with respect to public security personnel training, especially in the aspect of the consciousness, skills, and techniques of counterterrorism.[18] Chi Yannian emphasizes the slow response of counterterrorism forces in this instance and calls for the constant readiness of counterterrorism forces throughout China.[19]

Antiterrorist Preparations in China

Drawing lessons from the Mumbai terrorist attacks, China has been on high alert for possible terrorist attacks, especially during big events that catch the world's attention. Security measures for the 2008 Olympics were taken throughout the country several months before the Games opened. According to Meng Hongwei, deputy minister of the Ministry of Public Security, there were three main terrorist threats to the 2008 Olympic Games: international terrorists, terrorists from East Turkestan or separatists from Tibet, and various criminal elements. The second group, terrorists from East Turkestan, was accorded special priority.[20]

The Beijing 2008 Olympic Games and Shanghai World Expo 2010

In response to those potential terrorist threats, the three forces of the PLA joined together with local police in guaranteeing a safe Olympics. For the PLA, the core tasks were mainly nontraditional security threats, with an emphasis on the potential employment of nuclear or biochemical weapons.[21] The PLA Navy was responsible for insulating sea targets from terrorist attacks. In fulfilling this task, the navy had set up a multilayer observation and defense system for different sets of tasks, such as maritime patrol and surveillance, underwater security inspection and detection, maritime search and rescue, and emergencies under various circumstances.[22]

The three fleets of China's navy had their division of labor. A branch of the South China Sea Fleet was in charge of underwater security in the open waters around the "Bird's Nest," the Beijing National Stadium. It had a team of divers to conduct underwater routine inspections, removing suspicious objects.[23] The East China Sea Fleet and North China Sea Fleet coordinated offshore security during the Olympic Games. The sailing competition for the Olympic Games was held in Qingdao, which is also the headquarters for the North Sea Fleet. Its main responsibilities included patrol surveillance, undersea security inspections, search, and salvage. New-type equipment was also fielded by the North Sea Fleet and was deployed in a field exercise.

According to Huang Weichu, head of the nuclear, chemical, and biological emergency handling team and director of the disease control center of the Jinan Military Area Command, the employment of the new-type equipment raised the efficiency of reconnaissance and inspection by 83 percent.[24] The North Sea Fleet was also responsible for sailing-zone security inspections before it transferred the duty to local coast guard units a week before the opening of the Games.[25] In addition, a frigate group of the South Sea Fleet held formation tactical training in a complicated electromagnetic environment, ensuring the security of the Olympic events in Hong Kong. Finally, a submarine chaser group of the same fleet also organized a defensive formation for the Olympic security mission.[26]

The coast guard units around the coastal cities also participated actively in security measures for the Olympics. According to the 1st Brigade of the Guangdong coast guard, it had more than a thousand patrol missions within this period and effectively guaranteed security along the coast of Guangdong and Hong Kong. It also had all-weather, twenty-four-hour surveillance around the coast near Hong Kong.[27]

The World Expo was held in Shanghai during 2010. Security concerns were of top priority, and lessons learned from Mumbai were important to Expo security precautions.

Fishermen are rescued from their sinking vessel by a rescue helicopter of the China Maritime Safety Administration. Beijing has rapidly improved its search and rescue capabilities, but is also looking for assistance from Washington in this critical area of maritime nontraditional security.

The security measures taken were different from those of Beijing's Olympics, because the World Expo 2010 lasted longer, about five months, and Shanghai is a coastal city, with a coastline of 512 kilometers and twenty-one thousand square kilometers of sea area. Coastal security was accordingly a higher agenda item for this event. According to Hongkai Liu, Director General of Armed Policy of Shanghai and deputy commander for World Expo Security Headquarters, World Expo 2010 was different from most other world expos because of its location within the metropolitan area of Shanghai, rather than in rural areas or suburbs, which made security measures more complicated.[28]

Shanghai is a city with many big events, and the coastguardsmen there are quite skilled in security measures. Even so, formal training specifically for the World Expo 2010 began as early as March 2009, and related preparatory operations were completed much earlier. The three forces of the PLA also joined the security forces; a joint command headquarters was built in August 2009 and implemented 6 March 2010.[29]

Training for this event specifically focused on the prevention of destruction by terrorists of important targets at sea, prevention of potential explosions, and prevention of entanglement with local fishermen in coastal areas. New devices were deployed with Shanghai coast guard elements, including anti-explosive devices, interception guns, frogmen, and parachutists from helicopters. For the longer time span of World Expo 2010, coordinated efforts to draw security resources from neighboring municipalities were implemented, altogether encompassing eight provinces, together with Shanghai. New ships were built, especially including high-speed motorboats and patrol ships. The Chinese navy's East Sea Fleet coordinated with the coast guard to form an outer sea-security picket.[30]

Ongoing Efforts for International Coordination in the War against Terrorism

China is hardly alone in waging war against terrorists, and many international coordination efforts have been made in different programs, such as personnel training, joint exercises, information sharing, etc. For example, in the preparation of the 2008 Olympic Games in Beijing, many countries—including the United States, Israel, Britain, Australia, France, and Greece—joined efforts in lending expertise and assistance to ensure a safe and secure Olympics. There are reports that the United States exported some sophisticated equipment and technology to China for the first time and even sent a "nuclear accident response assistance group" to China.

Foreign experts also participated in training and mutual learning in China's antiterrorist efforts focused on the maritime flank, for example, in exchanges with both East Timor and Malaysia. The U.S. Coast Guard cutter *Rush* visited China and enhanced mutual understanding. In 2007, Capt. Bernard Moreland, USCG, lectured at the Ningbo China Coast Guard Academy for a week; he was the first Coast Guard officer from the United States to offer lectures at the Ningbo Academy.[31] China sends its security personnel abroad to such countries as France, Israel, Singapore, and Thailand for training.

Joint exercises among maritime forces are an important component of international coordination to enhance counterterrorism capabilities. China has participated actively in this kind of joint exercise—deploying not only the PLA Navy but also other sea forces, which include coast guard elements. As of 2009, there had been altogether twenty-eight joint military exercises conducted with PLA participation.[32]

On 22 October 2003, the PLA Navy and the Pakistani navy held a joint exercise codenamed DOLPHIN 0310 near an estuary of the Yangtze River in the East Sea. This was the first naval joint military exercise with a foreign counterpart in the nontraditional security field since the founding of the PLA Navy in 1949. The exercise included salvage on the sea, communications and information sharing, counterterrorism methods, and joint deployment. Later in 2003, a similar exercise was held with the Indian navy. China and Australia's first naval exercise was held in September 2004, and then–defense minister Robert Hill said in an interview that more efforts on information sharing and, especially, information relevant to counterterrorism should be made between the two navies. Since that time the PLA Navy has expanded the scope of its cooperation with other navies, frequently focusing on common, nontraditional maritime security threats. In addition, China's coast guard elements also engaged actively in international cooperation and mutual learning.

Connecting Locally: Civil-Naval Joint Exercise

To respond better to the challenges of nontraditional security issues and also to meet the needs of quick response in case of accidents, civil and naval joint efforts are needed. PLA Navy and civil maritime forces have been conducting joint exercises for the past few years.

On 26 May 2009 the first-ever large-scale civil-naval joint salvage exercise, LU HAI 2009, was held near the coasts of Fujian and Shandong. In this exercise, the Xiamen Salvage Call Center received a signal for help and shared this information with the nearby naval base, the Chinese coast guard, and thirteen other concerned departments. Altogether fifteen ships and one helicopter joined this exercise. On 9 July 2009 another civil-naval joint salvage exercise was held near the estuary of the Pearl River. Twenty-five ships and two helicopters from the South Sea Fleet, the South Sea Salvage Bureau, the South Sea Bureau of State Oceanic Administration, and Guangdong Customs joined this exercise.[33]

In the preparation of World Expo 2010, another civil-naval exercise, aiming at terrorist attacks, was held on 11 March 2010, in the East China Sea. This exercise mainly focused on countering possible terrorist attacks from the nearby sea and from ships passing by.[34] All those civil-naval salvage and antiterrorist exercises have built a better system for naval and civil forces to respond to the challenges posed by nontraditional security issues.

Conclusion: The Need for a Stronger, Multilayer "Great Wall" on the Sea

For the past sixty years, the PLA Navy has gone through several stages of development. This is true not only of the refinement and upgrading of equipment but more importantly of the guiding strategies of the PLA Navy. Many critics in China find that the PLA Navy has been preoccupied too much with near-coast responsibilities and that this tendency has constrained its efforts for an outgoing strategy. The Chinese navy should press farther out to the high seas. This seems especially urgent during the recent years, as China's interests overseas radically increase.

As for the coastal areas, some critics say other enforcement forces should handle most of the tasks in these areas. China does not have an integrated and powerful coast guard like the ones in such major sea powers as the United States and Japan. In recent years, there has been a call for an integrated and upgraded coast guard to perform more comprehensive near-coast duties, which are now performed by all "five dragons" (maritime enforcement agencies). With their overlaps and redundancies in performing certain duties, efficiencies have been lost.

To sum up, there is an urgent need for China to have enhanced coast guard forces to fulfill current challenges.[35] Stronger coast guard forces are needed by Beijing also to cope with tensions between China and Japan over the Diaoyu Islands, and between China and some East Asian countries over the South China Sea in late 2010 and early 2011. To meet those needs, enhanced international cooperation and confidence-building measures are needed. But cooperation and coordination in this field sometimes will be shaped and constrained by the ups and downs of China's foreign relationship in other fields, as shown in the suspension of ship-to-ship communication and intelligence sharing between China and the United States in the Gulf of Aden after the Obama administration's arms sale to Taiwan. Better coordination between China and the United States will prove to be of vital importance for both sides in promoting maritime security and reducing risks.

Notes

1. "中国共产党第十七次全国代表大会文件汇编" [Compilation of Seventeenth CCP National Congress Files], *People's Press,* 2007, p. 40.

2. Xiong Guangkai, "协力应对非传统安全威胁的新挑战" [Collaborating to Respond to New Challenges from Nontraditional Threats], 世界知识 [World Knowledge], no. 15 (2005), pp. 50–53; Tian Zhong, "海军非战争军事行动的特点、类型及能力建设" [Characteristics, Categories and Capability Development of Naval Nonwar Military Operations], 军事科学 [Military Science], no. 3 (2008), p. 25.

3. "The End of Mumbai Attack: Death Tolls Rise to 195," *China Daily,* 30 November 2008.

4. Raymond W. Kelly, *Lessons from the Mumbai Terrorist Attacks: Testimony before the Senate Committee on Homeland Security and Governmental Affairs,* 111th Cong., 1st sess., Washington, D.C., 8 January 2009, available at homeland.house.gov/.

5. "印度孟买恐怖袭击现五大特点" [Five Characteristics of Mumbai Terrorist Attacks in India], 人民网 [People's Daily Net], 27 November 2008, world.people.com.cn/GB/8421129.html.

6. "孟买袭击'震动'南亚几何" [The Mumbai Terrorist Attacks Have Deeply Shocked South Asia], 解放日报 [PLA Daily], 29 November 2008, available at news.xinhuanet.com/.

7. "谁是袭击的黑手?" [Who Are the Killers behind the Scene?], *Guangming Daily Organizer,* 5 December 2008, guancha.gmw.cn/.

8. "Mumbai Attack Gunman Qasab Sentenced to Death," *BBC News,* 6 May 2010, news.bbc.co.uk/.

9. "孟买恐怖袭击之后 印巴关系走向何方" [India-Pakistan Relations after Mumbai Attacks], *China Military Online,* 29 December 2008, www.chinamil.com.cn/.

10. Gao Tiejun, "Pakistan Sent 20,000 More Troops near the Border to India," Xinhua, 27 December 2008, news.xinhuanet.com.

11. "唯中国能制止印度对巴基斯坦报复战" [Only China Can Prevent India's Retaliation toward Pakistan], 西部网 [Western Net], 5 December 2008, mil.cnwest.com/content/2008-12/05/content_1616384.htm.

12. "印巴战争为何引而不发 全因中国军事压力" [No War Broke Out between India and Pakistan, All Due to China's Military Pressure], blog.huanqiu.com/?uid-860-action-viewspace-itemid-53288.

13. "伊朗总统内贾德: 孟买恐怖事件策划者或将袭击中国" [Warning from Iranian President Ahmadinejad: Terrorists Who Attacked Mumbai Are Plotting to Attack China], GCPnews.com, 3 December 2008.

14. "印恐怖袭击警示中国: 严防'东突'恐怖威胁" [Lessons Learned from Mumbai Terrorist Attacks That China Should Be Watchful at Threats by Terrorists from East Turkestan], *CCTV News,* news.cctv.com/.

15. Yao Yao, "对我国反恐情报工作的思考—从孟买恐怖袭击反思中国的反恐情报工作" [Reflections on Intelligence Work on China's Antiterrorist Preparation: Lessons Learned from Mumbai Terrorist Attacks], 铁道警官高等专科学校学报 [Journal of the Railway Police College], no. 4 (2009), pp. 74–77.

16. Li Wei, "孟买袭击案启示中国反恐" [Implications for China's Antiterrorist Preparation from the Mumbai Terrorist Attacks], Xinhua, 5 December 2008, news.xinhuanet.com/.

17. "Lack of Navy–Coast Guard Coordination Caused Mumbai Attacks," Indo-Asian News Service, 24 February 2009, available at www.hindustantimes.com/.

18. Xu Hao, "浅议孟买恐怖袭击事件对公安教育训练工作的启示" [Implications for the Training of Public Security Forces after Mumbai Terrorist Attacks], 上海公安高等专科学校学报 [Journal of Shanghai Policy College] 6 (2009), pp. 89–94.

19. Chi Yannian, "迟延年, 孟买恐怖袭击对反恐部队建设的启示" [Implications of Mumbai Terrorist for the Training of Antiterrorist Forces], 学习时报 [Study Times], 30 March 2009, p. 7.

20. "北京奥运会有三方面恐怖袭击威胁" [Three Major Threats Beijing Olympic Games Faced], Xinhua, 3 July 2007, news.xinhuanet.com/.

21. "东突恐怖组织" [East Turkestan Terrorist Organization], *China Military Online*, 9 July 2008, www.chinamil.com.cn/.

22. S. N. Pandey, *2008 Beijing Olympic Games: Scale, Composition and Force Mobilisation*, C3S Paper 211 (Chennai, India: Chennai Centre for China Studies, 7 October 2008), available at www.c3sindia.org/.

23. "Naval Frogmen to Remove Underwater Security Threats for Olympics," Xinhua, 5 December 2007, news.xinhuanet.com/.

24. Pandey, *2008 Beijing Olympic Games*.

25. "海军北海舰队筑牢奥运会海上安保屏障" [North Sea Fleets Formed Security Border on the Sea for Sailing Competition of Olympics], *PLA Daily*, 25 July 2008, www.chinamil.com.cn/.

26. Pandey, *2008 Beijing Olympic Games*.

27. "中国十万军警保卫奥运" [100,000 from the Army and Police Guarantee a Safe Olympics], 人民网 [People's Daily Net], 26 September 2008, military.people.com.cn/GB/8221/51755/119996/index.html.

28. "先进反恐装备将首次亮相世博" [Advanced Antiterrorist Equipment Has Its Debut in World Expo 2010], 人民网 [People's Daily Net], 13 March 2010, 2010lianghui.people.com.cn/GB/11135323.html.

29. "上海世博安保军队联合指挥部启用" [Headquarters for Joint Command for World Expo 2010 Put in Use], *PLA Daily*, 7 March 2010, military.people.com.cn/GB/1076/52984/11088904.html.

30. "东海舰队开展实兵对抗演练为世博会保驾护航" [East Sea Fleet Exercise for World Expo 2010], 环球时报 [Global Times], 10 October 2008, mil.huanqiu.com/china/2008-10/248916.html.

31. "美国海岸警卫队专家首次为中国海警官兵讲学" [First-Ever Expert from U.S. Coast Guard Lectures for Chinese Coast Guard], 王朝网络 [Dynasty Network], 22 June 2007, www.wangchao.net.cn/bbsdetail_940667.html.

32. "中国军队参加的28次主要中外联合军事演习" [The 28 Joint Military Exercises with PLA Participation], *Military People,* military.people.com.cn/GB/8221/69693/150099/161765/9681329.html.

33. "江口海域首次举行军地海上联合搜救演习" [Civil-Naval Joint Salvage Exercise First Held at Estuary of Pearl River], *China Today*, 9 July 2009, www.gov.cn/jrzg/2009-07/09/content_1361202.html.

34. "大规模军民联合海上反恐搜救综合演练成功举行" [Large Scale Civil-Military Joint Antiterrorist and Salvage Exercise on the Sea Successfully Held], *China Today*, 19 March 2010, www.gov.cn/jrzg/2010-03/19/content_1559415.htm.

35. He Zhonglong and Li Yunzhi, "组建我国海岸警卫队的必要性研究" [Research on the Necessity for Establishing the Coast Guard of China], 装备指挥技术学院学报 [Journal of the Academy of Equipment Command and Technology] 7, no. 2 (April 2006), pp. 10–13.

U.S. and Chinese Approaches to Peacekeeping and Stability Operations

Dennis J. Blasko

Many similarities exist in the way the governments of the United States and China prepare and organize for peacekeeping (PKO) and stability operations. Owing to differing threat environments and perceptions, national policies (including international commitments and alliances), physical and geographic conditions, force structures, and domestic political considerations, there are also important differences in the ways each country executes those missions. Nonetheless, peacekeeping and stability operations are major missions for the armed forces of both countries.

Perhaps the most significant similarity for both the United States and China is that their active-duty militaries are *not* tasked as the primary means of government power to maintain and enforce domestic stability. Other government organizations have that responsibility. However, both countries provide legal means for active-duty forces to *support* a variety of domestic security missions. The armed forces of both countries also actively prepare for, and are deployed in response to, a wide range of emergencies and natural disasters in accordance with national laws.

Definitions and Policy

The U.S. Department of Defense defines "peacekeeping" as "military operations undertaken *with the consent of all major parties* to a dispute, designed to monitor and facilitate implementation of an agreement."[1] A related term, "peace enforcement," does not require consent of the parties and is *generally* authorized by an international organization such as the UN, but the United States could act unilaterally if necessary or within a framework approved by an international organization other than the UN.

The United States has a long history, stretching back to 1950, of participating in military operations after UN Security Council authorization. It also participates in peacekeeping and peace-enforcement missions sanctioned by other international organizations, such as NATO. For example, the United States currently has deployed 1,480 troops to the NATO Kosovo Force (KFOR).

The Chinese term for peacekeeping is "maintaining peace operations" (维持和平行动). When referring to Chinese participation in these activities, the term is usually preceded by noting that the activities are sanctioned by the UN (联合国维持和平行动). This represents the first principle of Chinese participation in PKO missions—the requirement for UN authorization. To date, the Chinese have participated only in peacekeeping operations authorized by the UN Security Council and conducted under its auspices; some UN operations the Chinese have participated in have been authorized under Chapter VII of the UN Charter.

Beijing's long-standing, declared foreign policy seeks to avoid interference in the internal affairs of other countries, just as it seeks to prevent other countries from interfering with what it considers the internal affairs of China. UN authorization provides the Chinese government the legal justification it seeks potentially to "interfere in the internal affairs" of other nations.

China's policy toward peacekeeping operations was defined in its first white paper on national defense, published in 1998. In addition to emphasizing the necessity of the UN mandate, this statement underlined that "in peace-keeping operations, the following principles, which have proved to be effective in the past, should be adhered to: obtaining agreement from the country concerned beforehand, strictly observing neutrality and prohibiting the use of force except for self-defense."[2]

Over the past twenty years, as China has increased its participation in UN peacekeeping missions, Beijing has adhered to these principles. Currently, views about peacekeeping in Beijing and Washington have become closer, but they are still not completely congruent (as demonstrated by Chinese reluctance to participate in any but UN-sanctioned missions). A much larger difference in definitions is found in the term "stability operations."

The Pentagon defines "stability operations" as "an overarching term encompassing various military missions, tasks, and activities *conducted outside the United States* in coordination with other instruments of national power to maintain or reestablish a safe and secure environment, provide essential governmental services, emergency infrastructure reconstruction, and humanitarian relief" [emphasis supplied]. The key element here is "conducted outside the United States," which means that the U.S. military does not consider actions it undertakes inside the United States as "stability operations." Many of these functions could be called military operations other than war (MOOTW), peacekeeping, peace enforcement, or nation building. U.S. military forces have been deployed both legally and routinely within the United States to conduct many operations that fall within the parameters above.

The U.S. military recently has been engaged in a variety of these actions in Iraq and Afghanistan. Moreover, American doctrine foresees the potential for more such missions in the future. As noted in the foreword to the U.S. Army field manual on stability operations, "The greatest threat to our national security comes not in the form of terrorism or ambitious powers, but from fragile states either unable or unwilling to provide for the most basic needs of their people."[3] Recognizing that it was involved in multiple "stability operations" and would be for a long to come, in November 2005 the Department of Defense (DoD) issued a directive that emphasized that "stability operations were no longer secondary to combat operations."[4] This was a major change in U.S. military doctrine, resulting from realities of the past decade, and one that has not yet quite been replicated by the PLA.

The roles and missions of the Chinese armed forces are defined in article 22 of the 1997 National Defense Law. The law mandates the PLA is to be externally oriented but that as a secondary mission it may assist in maintaining public order. At the same time, the primary mission of the People's Armed Police (PAP) is domestic security. The militia supports both internal and external missions.

The Chinese military considers preparing to fight a local war under informationized conditions as its *core mission*, with preparation for and execution of "nontraditional security," "nonwar," or "nonmilitary" missions as an important adjunct but not with an equal priority, as in U.S. doctrine. As stated in a March 2010 article in the military newspaper *Jiefangjun Bao (Liberation Army Daily)*:

> Our military's historic mission for the new stage of the new century requires us not only to win local wars under the condition of informatization but also to carry out nonmilitary operations.... However, no] matter how the security situation changes, how the military's functions broaden, ... curbing [deterring] war, winning wars and maintaining peace are always the most fundamental duty of our military."[5]

The main nonwar military actions include a wide array of missions—for example, antiterrorism, domestic stability, border control, emergency response (such as for a public health crisis), disaster relief, search and rescue, peacekeeping, and nuclear, biological, and chemical (NBC) defense.[6]

As seen in this task list and from many recent actual deployments, all elements of the Chinese armed forces may be called on to perform both domestic and external traditional security and nontraditional security missions. For domestic stability requirements, such as handling "sudden incidents" (突发事件), and antiterrorist operations, the civilian police and PAP are the government's first and second lines of defense, respectively, with the PLA as a third line, providing support as required.

Perhaps the best example of civilian police–PLA–PAP–militia cooperation was seen in the 2008 Olympic security procedures implemented throughout China. Overall security was the responsibility of the multiministry, civilian-led Beijing Olympic Security

Coordination Group. Within the Beijing Olympic Security Command Center, led by Beijing Municipality police chief Ma Zhenchuan, PLA participation was supervised by a Military Work (or Affairs) Bureau headed by Senior Col. Tian Yixiang.[7] The PLA provided air defense and coastal security, as well as backup antiterrorist and NBC support, for all Olympic venues. In total, the PLA contributed "46,000 troops, 98 fixed-wing aircraft, 60 helicopters, 63 ships, and some ground-to-air missiles, and radar, chemical defense and engineering support equipment" to the Olympic security network throughout the country. The PAP provided some 85,000 troops to the effort.[8] Despite these large numbers from the PLA and PAP, civilian police forces nonetheless had primary responsibility for site security and initial response.

Organization and Command and Control

Policies for peacekeeping and stability operations are formulated at the national level for both the United States and Chinese armed forces. Within the former, the Deputy Assistant Secretary of Defense (DASD) for Partnership Strategy and Stability advises "the Department's leadership on all matters pertaining to stabilization and reconstruction operations, foreign disaster relief, humanitarian assistance, international peacekeeping efforts and non-combatant evacuations."[9] In China, two offices share these same responsibilities in two ostensibly different headquarters in Beijing. Within the Ministry of National Defense (MND), a Peacekeeping Affairs Office (国防部维和事务办公室) was "established in 2001 to oversee the strategic management and coordination of the PLA's participation in UN peacekeeping operations."[10] Unlike in the United States, the Chinese defense minister is not in the chain of command for the armed forces (though he is a member of the Central Military Commission). The role of the Chinese MND is related mainly to "exchanges in the military field with foreign institutions";[11] it also exercises oversight of peacekeeping (through the Peacekeeping Affairs Office).[12]

(Currently the director of the MND Peacekeeping Affairs Office is Maj. Gen. Shi Zhengbo.[13] The MND website has a "Peacekeeping" webpage [eng.mod.gov.cn/Peacekeeping/index.htm] that includes introductory information, photographs, and links to recent articles about Chinese participation in UN peacekeeping missions.)

Primary responsibility for handling day-to-day tasks for most other nonwar or nontraditional security missions, including antiterrorism, disaster relief, and support to internal security missions, resides in the General Staff Department (GSD) Operations Department Emergency Office (解放军总参谋部作战部应急办). (The office director is Senior Col. Tian Yixiang—the same Senior Colonel Tian who was in charge of PLA support to Olympic security.)[14]

The Emergency Office was established in 2003 and is a division-leader-grade-level organization, with about twenty personnel. During emergencies, such as the Wenchuan earthquake, and for scheduled support to internal security missions, such as the Olympics, Senior Colonel Tian is a major player in coordinating with other Chinese government organizations and supervising military actions. Senior Colonel Tian executes the decisions made by the Leading Group Office for Responding to Emergencies established within the GSD when needed.[15] The exact composition of this leading group varies according to the crisis at hand.

In January 2006, a Chinese "national plan on emergency response," complete with color-coded alert system, was announced. This plan outlines government preparation for unexpected incidents, social stability, natural disasters, accidents, public health, and social safety. The plan designates a State Council "office in charge of emergency response management to collect information on various incidents and co-ordinate response work." In particular, "the army and police will provide major task forces dealing with emergencies," responding to civilian, not military, authority. For incidents outside China involving Chinese citizens or organizations, such as commercial companies, "Chinese embassies and relevant State Council departments and regional governments should organize emergency relief work."[16] This last clause specifies that Beijing prefers that local foreign governments take the lead in emergency actions involving Chinese citizens in their countries, including reacting to terrorist incidents. At this time, the Chinese government is not anxious to deploy its security forces overseas to resolve hostage situations.

In the event of terrorist activities inside China, national-level coordination will be headed by a small group in the Central Committee of the Chinese Communist Party, with its headquarters in the Ministry of Public Security, where the National Anti-Terrorist Command Center has been established. The civilian police would provide the primary antiterrorist response force, backed up by PAP antiterrorist units and supported by appropriate PLA forces as necessary.[17] The preference for civilian police forces to be used to control domestic security situations is consistent with the national emergency plan and is also explained in other official government documents.

For example, in the 2006 defense white paper the PAP's chain of command for internal security operations is described as follows: "In terms of *conducting public security operations* (执行公安任务) . . . the [PAP] General Headquarters is *under the leadership and command of the Ministry of Public Security,* and the [PAP] units at and below the contingent level are under the leadership and command of the *public security organs at the same level.*"[18] This quote specifies civilian command for public security functions, such as crowd-control or antiriot operations, at both the national and local levels, in routine and emergency situations. Left unstated by the white paper is the fact that PLA units may assist or provide support to such operations, as defined in the National Defense Law. In the years since 1989 such assistance has been limited, with the most visible example occurring in March 2008 in Lhasa, where local PLA units were deployed to man checkpoints and conduct patrols—*after* the police and PAP had restored order.

In general, the Chinese chain of command for responding to terrorist incidents inside and outside China parallels the American system. Inside the United States, the Department of Justice and the Federal Bureau of Investigation, along with local jurisdictions, have primary responsibility for responding to terrorism, while in the case of terrorist incidents overseas, the U.S. embassy and Department of State take the lead.

In September 2009, Senior Colonel Tian wrote an article for *Jiefangjun Bao* about the PLA "emergency command mechanism" responsible for the deployment of PLA and PAP units during "emergency rescue and disaster relief operations." In it he notes that the mechanism was established in March 2005 as a "coordinated military-civil joint action mechanism," which includes information sharing.[19] In order to respond to MOOTW requirements, on 5 January 2009 the GSD issued the "Plan on PLA's Capacity Building in Military Operations Other than War," specifying guidelines, principles, and objectives, as well as the size and strength of and measures for building MOOTW forces.[20] Five types of dedicated emergency-response and peacekeeping units (not including antiterrorist units) were later identified:[21]

- Nineteen flood relief units from the PLA engineering force
- An earthquake emergency rescue force, consisting of PLA engineering troops and medical workers from the PAP, known as the China International Search and Rescue Team and China Emergency Fire Rescue Team[22]
- Emergency rescue forces for nuclear, chemical, and biological disasters, consisting of chemical defense troops from the military regions and medical rescue workers from the Academy of Military Medical Sciences
- Ten transportation and communications emergency relief groups, consisting of engineering units from the army engineering force and the Second Artillery
- International peacekeeping force amounting to at least "one UN standard engineering battalion, one UN standard medical team and two UN standard transportation companies."[23]

These emergency-response units have been issued special equipment for their missions and receive special training. Their expertise will be augmented with manpower and logistics support from units in the local area, as well as by civilian support. In many cases, the first units responding to natural disasters will be from local PAP and militia or reserve units. Reports of civil-military training in all these missions throughout the country are common.

In the wake of the Yushan earthquake of April 2010, Senior Colonel Tian said, "The armed forces have done better and acted quicker than they did during the Wenchuan quake relief."[24] He also announced that eight "state-level [national-level] specialized emergency rescue units," with a total of fifty thousand personnel, would be formed and become operational by the end of 2010. "Regulations of the PLA on Emergency Command in Handling Contingencies" will also be issued soon.[25] This appears to be a centralization of emergency response units under GSD control, which could eliminate several levels of command, while likely maintaining their decentralized distribution throughout the country.

For counterterrorism operations, every military region, the navy, and the air force's 15th Airborne Army each have a special operations group with subordinate elements trained in antiterrorism tactics. Any of these units could cooperate with a variety of PAP antiterrorist units and Ministry of Public Security (MPS) antiterrorist squads found in most major cities. There is no indication at this time that the PLA intends to consolidate these decentralized special operations units (each of about a thousand personnel) into a national-level command organization. So far, no dedicated air units (fixed-wing or rotary-wing) have been assigned in full-time support to special operations.

As in the PLA, a number of U.S. forces are tasked to be contingency forces for a variety of stability-related missions. However, they are much more centrally controlled and organized than in the PLA. On 1 October 2002 the U.S. Northern Command (USNORTHCOM) was established to provide command and control over DoD's homeland-defense efforts and to coordinate Defense support of civilian authorities.[26] In addition to having responsibility for aerospace warning and control, USNORTHCOM commands a dedicated drug-interdiction task force, forces guarding the national capital, a U.S. Army brigade on call for emergencies, and a task force dedicated to the threat of weapons of mass destruction.

In contrast to the long experience of the U.S. armed forces in expeditionary, joint warfare, the Chinese armed forces have only about ten years of training and organization as "modular, versatile, and rapidly deployable" forces and minimal experience in operating beyond China's borders. To date, their experience has mostly been in conducting exercises and operations within China or just outside. The 2008 deployment of 146,000 active-duty PLA and PAP personnel, plus 75,000 reservists and militia, in response to the Wenchuan earthquake was the largest deployment of Chinese armed forces since the 1979 border war with Vietnam.[27] As for overseas deployments, in addition to the PLA Navy's antipiracy deployment to the Gulf of Aden, small units of PLA and PAP forces from all over the country have had the opportunity to be tested in real-world peacekeeping operations in Africa, Asia, and North America. They provide benefit to the UN PKO missions to which they are assigned, as they gain experience in long-distance

Current Chinese Peacekeeping Operations

China has deployed personnel to UN peacekeeping missions since about 1990. As of 28 February 2010, China ranked fourteenth among all contributors to UN PKO missions, with 2,137 military and civilian police personnel deployed to ten missions (see figure 1). Of the five permanent members of the UN Security Council, China contributes the largest number of personnel. In comparison, France ranks sixteenth, with 1,673 personnel; Russia is forty-second, with 362; the United Kingdom is forty-sixth, with 275; and the United States ranks number seventy-one, with eighty-six personnel deployed to seven UN PKO missions.[28] The United States and China both contribute personnel to missions in Haiti, the Congo, Liberia, Sudan, and the Middle East.

Figure 1. *Chinese and U.S. Participation in UN PKO Missions (February 2010)*
Source: "UN Mission's Summary Detailed by Country," *United Nations*, 28 February 2010, www.un.org/.

Mission	Experts on Mission	Individual Police*	Formed Police Unit**	Contingent Troop	Total Chinese	Total U.S.
MINURSO (Western Sahara)	11				11	
MINUSTAH (Haiti)	16		126		142	53
MONUC (Congo)	16			218	234	2
UNAMID (Darfur)	2			322	324	
UNIFIL (Lebanon)				344	344	
UNMIL (Liberia)	2	14		565	581	19
UNMIS (Sudan)	12	11		444	467	6
UNMIT (Timor-Leste)	2	22			24	
UNOCI (Côte d'Ivoire)	7				7	
UNTSO (Middle East)	3				3	2

* "Individual police" are Ministry of Public Security police.
** "Formed police units" consist of MPS antiriot police and PAP border-defense antiriot police personnel.

Approximately 115 countries make available over a hundred thousand personnel for sixteen UN missions. Bangladesh, Pakistan, and India are the three largest contributors of personnel, with over ten thousand each for Bangladesh and Pakistan and over eight thousand for India. China is in the second tier of twenty-two countries, each providing from one to five thousand personnel. About eighty nations contribute fewer than a thousand personnel. Thus with about 2 percent of the overall personnel, China is a significant contributor but is still a long way from the top of personnel providers.

As seen in figure 2, when each mission is examined individually China provides from 0.1 to over 5 percent of the personnel total. In no case does China provide the largest number of personnel per mission, and it usually trails the leading contributing country by a wide margin. As such, China's participation is useful but not crucial to the missions.

Figure 2. *Percentage of Chinese Personnel Compared to Mission Total*
Source: "UN Mission's Summary Detailed by Country," *United Nations,* 28 February 2010, www.un.org/.

Mission	Total Chinese	Total from All Countries	Percentage Chinese	Largest Contributor/ Number of Personnel	Total Number of Countries Contributing
MINURSO (Western Sahara)	11	224	4.9	Malaysia/20	29
MINUSTAH (Haiti)	142	9,087	1.6	Brazil/1,282	48
MONUC (Congo)	234	20,573	1.1	India/4,552	57
UNAMID (Darfur)	324	21,800	1.5	Nigeria/3,843	48
UNIFIL (Lebanon)	344	11,504	3.0	Italy/2,236	31
UNMIL (Liberia)	581	10,427	5.6	Pakistan/3,109	60
UNMIS (Sudan)	467	10,541	4.4	India/2,706	68
UNMIT (Timor-Leste)	24	1,521	1.6	Malaysia/216	40
UNOCI (Côte d'Ivoire)	7	8,544	0.1	Bangladesh/2,345	53
UNTSO (Middle East)	3	153	2.0	Finland/14	23

The PLA contributes battalion-sized units to five missions, and PAP border-defense units contribute antiriot police personnel to the mission in Haiti. For the PLA, deployments are centered on an engineer battalion, with medical support, and often a transportation unit. As seen in figure 3, units from all over the country provide forces. So far, in contrast to the United States, the PLA has not committed infantry or armored combat forces to UN PKO missions.

Units undergo predeployment training and then are deployed for eight months at a time. Often they deploy in batches, with half the force arriving for an overlap period with the

Figure 3. *Major PLA and PAP Contributions*

Source: Multiple news articles; "Backgrounder: Main Distribution of Current Chinese Peacekeepers," Xinhua, 19 January 2010, news.xinhuanet.com/.

Mission	Number of Deployments/ Start Date	Source of Troops	Type/Size Units (# of personnel may vary)
MINUSTAH (Haiti)	8/Oct. 2004	PAP Yunnan and Guangdong Border Defense units; Xinjiang Border Defense unit; Shandong Border Defense unit; Fujian Border Defense unit (some units have provided troops more than once; sometimes deployed with MPS antiriot police)	Antiriot police (125)
MONUC (Congo)	11/April 2003	Lanzhou MR; Beijing MR Engineer Brigade (2004)	Engineer battalion (175); Medical (43)
UNAMID (Darfur)	3/Nov. 2007	Jinan MR; Beijing MR	Engineer battalion (315); Medical (7)
UNIFIL (Lebanon)	6/March 2006	Chengdu MR/13th Group Army	Engineer battalion (275); Medical (60)
UNMIL (Liberia)	10/Dec. 2003	Beijing MR Engineer Brigade, Inner Mongolia MD, and unidentified group army; Shenyang and Nanjing MRs (2004)	Engineer battalion (275); Transportation battalion (240); Medical (43)
UNMIS (Sudan)	6/Sept. 2005	Jinan MR (including personnel from an armored division)	Engineer battalion (275); Transportation company (100); Medical (60)

force it relieves. All of these missions have seen multiple deployments and redeployments of forces, and it is not unusual for individual soldiers to have served multiple tours, perhaps on multiple missions.

As much as two months of predeployment training is conducted at unit garrisons before personnel go to formal PAP and PLA peacekeeping training facilities. The PAP established the China Peacekeeping CIVPOL Training Center (CPCTC) in August 2000 in Langfang, Hebei Province, where it trains both Chinese and foreign civilian-police peacekeepers. The center has been expanded since its founding.[29] PLA troops train at the Nanjing Political Academy (for language and general skill training) and at the newly established MND Peacekeeping Center at Huairou, in Beijing Municipality.[30] It appears that PLA and PAP personnel do not train together.

For the Haiti mission, PAP border-defense antiriot police work in conjunction with MPS antiriot police from different parts of the country. Individual antiriot-police personnel are selected from their larger units and deployed as "formed police units" for the length of their rotations. Haiti represents the only deployment of PAP forces on UN PKO missions. Following the earthquake in Haiti in January 2010, ten Chinese peacekeepers and two squads from the U.S. 82nd Airborne Division conducted at least one joint patrol, in conjunction with the Haitian special police in Port-au-Prince.[31]

So far only one UN PKO mission has been commanded by a PLA officer. In August 2007, Maj. Gen. Zhao Jingmin was designated force commander for the United Nations Mission for the Referendum in Western Sahara (MINURSO). (Prior to that assignment Zhao had served in MINURSO from 1991 to 1992, in the United Nations Iraq-Kuwait Observation Mission from 1996 to 1997, and in the MND Peacekeeping Affairs Office from 2003 to 2007.)[32]

With regard to funding, the UN PKO budget for 2010 is about $7.9 billion. The leading contributors are the United States, with 27.17 percent, and Japan, with 12.53 percent. The United Kingdom, Germany, France, and Italy form a second tier, contributing between 5 and 8 percent, while China is at the top of the third tier, with 3.94 percent.[33] This amounts to about $311 million for China, up from $270 million in 2007. Given the size of China's GDP, it would seem that an increase in this number should not cause excessive strain on the Chinese government's budget. Equally, there is little doubt that were the Chinese political and military leadership to determine it to be in its interest, the PLA could greatly increase the number of troops deployed to UN PKO missions, including the addition of combat forces. An important question, though, is how a decision to deploy PLA combat troops on overseas peacekeeping missions would be received by foreign governments.

Conclusions

There is no question that the Chinese armed forces have embraced nontraditional security measures as a major mission and a factor in force building and training. Still, preparing for and deterring local war remains the PLA's core mission, unlike the U.S. armed forces, where stability operations have the same priority as combat operations. Just as equipping the large PLA active-duty force with sufficient modern weapons and information technologies to prosecute integrated joint combat operations is a challenge, the tasks of adequately equipping the force with the specialized equipment necessary for disaster-relief operations and stockpiling supplies in dispersed locations reasonably near areas of need are also problematic. Likewise, conducting realistic training for war and nonwar missions will continue to be time-consuming, expensive, and difficult. Because of different technological levels among units within the forces, it is likely that, for both war and nonwar missions, relatively small numbers of highly trained, advanced units will be integrated with much larger numbers of less well equipped forces to work in tandem to accomplish the mission.

Chinese People's Armed Police patrol in the northwest frontier province of Xinjiang. The Chinese armed forces, including the PLA, continue to view domestic security as well as disaster relief missions, such as operations related to the 2008 earthquake in Sichuan, as core duties.

In the event of emergencies and war, units from all the armed forces will work closely with civilian counterparts, who in many nonwar scenarios will actually be in the lead. Similarly, high technology will be combined with massive manual labor to perform many tasks. A recent example of this in the Chinese context was modern Il-76 transport aircraft flying into remote disaster regions only to be unloaded by chains of men lugging cargo on their backs, instead of by palletized cargo systems found in other militaries.

With regard to terrorist and hostage situations involving Chinese citizens and interests overseas, the record is clear that in fact Beijing pursues a policy in which "Chinese embassies and relevant State Council departments" work with regional governments to "organize emergency relief work." A quick review of several incidents of Chinese nationals taken hostage in recent years reveals that nearly all have been released after the Chinese dispatched government officials to work with local governments and civic organizations to negotiate terms of release. These terms are usually not made public. The only armed rescue attempted by a foreign government resulted in a dead hostage. There is no evidence in any of the nine incidents reviewed for this study of the Chinese government threatening to use force to free its people.[34]

Beijing is driven to follow this policy in part because of the limitations of its antiterrorist forces, the lack of strategic mobility to get its forces in place rapidly, and shortfalls in collecting the detailed intelligence necessary for a successful hostage rescue or antiterrorist mission. The Chinese government's acceptance of these realities appears generally to have resulted in the successful release of its citizens.

In the summer of 2009, during the visit of the Chief of Staff of the U.S. Army to Beijing, the Chinese suggested the prospect of conducting bilateral humanitarian-assistance and disaster-relief training.[35] However, the overall political climate between the countries did not permit agreement on the topic for two years. After a period of cool military-to-military relations, in July 2011 the U.S. and Chinese armed forces agreed, during the visit of the chairman of the Joint Chiefs of Staff to China, to conduct several combined humanitarian-assistance/disaster-relief exercises in 2011 and 2012. A press release stated that "hospital ships of the two navies will conduct exchanges and carry out joint medical and rescue drills [but no date for the exercise was given] . . . armed forces from both sides will conduct joint humanitarian rescue and disaster relief drills in the third quarter of 2012 . . . [and] the two navies will also carry out joint anti-piracy drills in the Gulf of Aden in the fourth quarter of [2011]."[36] Such exercises likely will be very simple at first, but potentially could expand to more complex operations.

Despite the disruptions in the China-U.S. military-to-military relationship, as Chinese armed forces continue to engage in peacekeeping and stability-related operations overseas it is increasingly likely that they will come in contact with U.S. forces. As demonstrated in Haiti on the smallest of scales, professional military and paramilitary personnel can cooperate and execute operations that benefit the overall mission and contribute to improved relations between the two armed forces. The United States and China will often share national interests in contributing to peacekeeping and stability operations in foreign lands. Increased knowledge and awareness of each other's doctrines and capabilities will help realize those mutual interests.

Notes

1. U.S. Defense Dept., *Department of Defense Dictionary of Military and Associated Terms*, JP 1-02 (Washington, D.C.: 8 November 2010 [as amended through 15 November 2011]), available at www.dtic.mil/ [emphasis added].

2. People's Republic of China [hereafter PRC], *China's National Defense* (Beijing: Information Officer of the State Council, July 1998), sec. IV, available at www.china.org.cn/e-white/5/5.4.htm#4.

3. U.S. Army Dept., *Stability Operations*, FM 3-07 (Washington, D.C.: October 2008), foreword.

4. Ibid., p. vi.

5. "Commentator on Hu Jintao's Speech to PLA Delegation to NPC (2)," *Jiefangjun Bao* [Liberation Army Daily] *Online* [in Chinese], 21 March 2010, p. 1, trans. Open Source Center [hereafter OSC], CPP20100322710001.

6. "Diversified Military Tasks Not Equal to Nonwar Military Actions," summary, *Zhongguo Guofang Bao Online* [in Chinese], 11 December 2008, trans. OSC, CPP20081212088003.

7. "Chinese Military Preparing for Beijing Olympic Security," *People's Daily*, 29 June 2007, english.peopledaily.com.cn/.

8. All Olympic security figures come from *China's National Defense in 2008* (Beijing: January 2009), available at english.gov.cn/official/2009-01/20/content_1210227_12.htm.

9. "Assistant Secretary of Defense for Special Operations/Low Intensity Conflict," *U.S. Defense Dept.*, policy.defense.gov/solic/.

10. Bates Gill and Chin-Hao Huang, *China's Expanding Role in Peacekeeping: Prospects and Policy Implications*, SIPRI Policy Paper 25 (Solna, Swed.: November 2009), p. 5.

11. See "Organizations of the Central Military Commission (CMC)," available on the official website of the Chinese government at english.gov.cn/2005-09/02/content_28477.htm.

12. Ibid.

13. References to Shi Zhengbo are found at Hu Yue, "China Plays a Bigger Role in International Peacekeeping Efforts," *Beijing Review*, 28 January 2010, available at china-wire.org/?p=4691.

14. There are many references to Senior Colonel Tian including "国防部首次在开放部队举办新闻发布会"[China's Defense Ministry Holds Its First-Ever Conference on News Publication] 中国军网 [China Military Online], 2 August 2008, available at www.chinamil.com.cn/site1/xwpdxw/2008-08/02/content_1392392.htm. Ma Jian is identified at "Official: Five in Copter Crash Only Military Quake Relief Deaths," 中国军网 [China Military Online], 12 June 2008, available at english.chinamil.com.cn/site2/special-reports/2008-06/12/content_1312074.htm.

15. "PLA Emergency Command Mechanism Shows High Efficiency," *Jiefangjun Bao Online* [in English], 23 September 2009, trans. OSC, CPP20090924702004.

16. "Emergency Response Guidelines Announced," *People's Daily*, 9 January 2006, english.peopledaily.com.cn/.

17. "Chinese President Calls for Enhanced Antiterrorism Effort," *People's Daily*, 24 January 2006, english.peopledaily.com.cn/200601/24/eng20060124_237714.html; conversations in Beijing in April 2010 with knowledgeable PLA officers.

18. PRC, *China's National Defense in 2006* (Beijing: Information Officer of the State Council, December 2006), sec. V, available at www.china.org.cn/english/features/book/194480.htm [emphasis supplied].

19. "PLA Emergency Command Mechanism Shows High Efficiency."

20. "State-Level Specialized Emergency Rescue Troops to Be Established by Late 2010," *PLA Daily*, 21 April 2009, available at eng.chinamil.com.cn/.

21. "PLA Constructs MOOTW Arms Force System," *PLA Daily*, 14 May 2009, available at eng.mod.gov.cn/.

22. "新闻背景: 中国国际救援队" [News Background: China International Search and Rescue Team], Xinhua, 9 October 2005, news.xinhuanet.com/.

23. PRC, *China's National Defense in 2002* (Beijing: Information Officer of the State Council, December 2002), available at english.gov.cn/official/2005-07/28/content_17780.htm.

24. "Chinese Armed Forces Provide Quick Response, Quake Relief to Yushu," *PLA Daily*, 21 April 2010, eng.chinamil.com.cn/.

25. "State-Level Specialized Emergency Rescue Troops to Be Established by Late 2010."

26. R. Barry Cronin, *U.S. Northern Command & Defense Support of Civil Authorities*, Newsletter 10-16 (Fort Leavenworth, Kans.: U.S. Army Combined Arms Center, Center for Army Lessons Learned, December 2009), usacac.army.mil/.

27. *China's National Defense in 2008*.

28. United Nations, "Ranking of Military and Police Contributions to UN Operations," *United Nations Peacekeeping*, 28 February 2020, www.un.org/.

29. "A Brief Introduction to China Peacekeeping CIVPOL Training Center," 23 November 2006, *Chinese Ministry of Public Security*, www.mps.gov.cn/n16/n983040/n1372264/n1372567/1501154.html; "UN Keen on More Peacekeepers," *People's Daily*, 21 November 2007, english.peopledaily.com.cn/.

30. "China Plays Its Peacekeeping Role," *China Daily*, 29 June 2009, www.chinadaily.com.cn/.

31. "China, US Peacekeepers Conduct Joint Patrol in Haiti," *China Daily*, 29 January 2010, www.chinadaily.com.cn/.

32. "Secretary-General Appoints Major General Zhao Jingmin of China as Force Commander for Western Sahara Mission," Biographical Note SG/A/1089 BIO/3918, *United Nations*, 28 August 2007, www.un.org/.

33. "Background Note: United Nations Peacekeeping," *United Nations*, funding chart, www.un.org/en/peacekeeping/documents/backgroundnote.pdf.

34. These incidents include Iraq (April 2004 and January 2005), Pakistan (October 2004), Nigeria (January 2007, February 2007, and May 2010),

Cameroon (March 2010), and Yemen (May 2010), in addition to the capture of the Chinese vessel *De Xin Hai* (December 2009).

35. Charlie Reed, "Casey: U.S., China to Begin Joint Humanitarian Relief Training," *Stars and Stripes,* 26 August 2009.

36. "China, U.S. Announce Military Exchange Plans," *China Military Online,* 12 July 2011, eng.chinamil.com.cn/.

CHAPTER NINE

On China-U.S. Relations and NTS Cooperation

Maj. Gen. Pan Zhenqiang, People's Liberation Army (Ret.)

China-U.S. relations seem to have come across troubles again. This time, the clear drivers for the new round of tussles between the two powers are the recent high-profile demonstrations of American military muscle in East Asia, which were unmistakably targeted against the so-called rise of China. But to many Chinese pundits, the eagerness of the Obama administration to demonstrate its tough hand is also a reflection of a sort of strategic anxiety of the United States over its predicaments both at home and abroad, whether real or imagined.

To be sure, as he looks around the world, President Obama has enough reasons to be unhappy with himself. He has been overburdened with so many thorny domestic issues and frustrated with so many setbacks in carrying out international commitments. When the country is engulfed in an overwhelming pessimism about its future, the United States tends to be defensive, desperate to want to take measures to consolidate its dominance over global as well as regional affairs. Mishandled, this sentiment could be one of the significant factors that will bear on the evolution of the China-U.S. relations in the future.

The present paper seeks to elaborate on what the two powers should do to overcome this unhealthy psychology to keep their bilateral relationship on the right track. Among many other suggestions, the paper highlights one point—that is, while the two powers continue to be constrained in the traditional security field, promoting nontraditional security cooperation could be very conducive and timely to the maintenance of a stable and cooperative relationship between the two great nations.

I

The China policy of the Obama administration has taken a strange course. Unlike his predecessors, President Obama seemed to demonstrate unusual enthusiasm for a more cooperative relationship with China at the very outset of his presidency. Under his guidance, and thanks to joint efforts, the two countries seemed immediately to enter a warm period, in which the two sides expanded their engagement and cooperation in almost all political, economic, and security fields in the first year of the Obama administration. In Washington, there was even a whisper of a prospect of "G-2"—meaning China-U.S. cooperative governance of global affairs. Although that prediction has never

Secretary of Defense Robert Gates and Deputy Chief of the PLA General Staff General Ma Xiaotian share a light moment. Nevertheless, the bilateral security relationship is still plagued with mistrust, unfortunately. Active cooperation in the domain of nontraditional security could help to build more constructive relationships and thus help to alleviate this persistent problem.

been appealing to the Chinese side, the two powers did succeed in reaching a joint statement when President Obama visited Beijing in November 2009. The document was the culmination of an extensive new consensus between the two state leaders and was supposed to provide a set of new guiding principles and a roadmap toward building a sustained, cooperative China-U.S. bilateral relationship in the post–Cold War era. The two countries agreed on the nature of this most important bilateral relationship as they reiterated that "they are committed to building a positive, cooperative and comprehensive China-US relationship for the 21st century, and will take concrete actions to steadily build a partnership to address common challenges."[1]

The joint statement also explicitly recognized the importance of strengthening mutual confidence and trust for China-U.S. relations in the new era. There is a particular paragraph that stresses the right approach to that end:

> The two sides reiterated that the fundamental principle of respect for each other's sovereignty and territorial integrity is at the core of the three Sino-U.S. joint communiqués that guide China-U.S. relations. Neither side supports any attempts by any force to undermine this principle. The two sides agreed that respecting each other's core interests is extremely important to ensure steady progress in China-US relations.[2]

To many Chinese, the joint statement would constitute a document of milestone significance if truly implemented. In their view, it has not only provided a strong political basis for a sound China-U.S. cooperative relationship in the future but, more importantly, recorded American acceptance that "respecting each other's core interests is extremely important to ensure steady progress in China-US relations." This meant to many Chinese a virtual acceptance for the first time on the part of the United States of China as a partner on an equal basis and a respect for China's national core interests in the bilateral interaction. The perception led to an expectation in China that the major obstacle to bilateral cooperation between the two great nations had been removed and that a new vista would open up for the China-U.S. cooperation.

That expectation soon fell apart. After his return to Washington from the Beijing trip, President Obama seemed immediately to show the other side of his face. He announced a $6.4 billion weapon sale to Taiwan. As if that were not enough to offend the Chinese, he decided to meet with the Dalai Lama at the White House when the latter visited Washington in February 2010. From Beijing's perspective, both acts amounted to wanton trampling on China's core national interests, virtually a stab in its back, particularly given the just concluded joint statement. The Chinese government angrily responded with a strong protest and cut off all the intended military-to-military contacts. The indignant Chinese public felt betrayed by Obama, whose credibility in China plummeted almost overnight.

One plausible explanation for Obama's abrupt about-face is that he may well have been hijacked by the Washington establishment. Despite his wish for better cooperation in China-U.S. relations, he could not resist the great pressure of those from the Pentagon, State Department, and Congress, not to mention the anti-China media and think tanks, among many others in Washington who believed that his visit to Beijing had been a humiliation to the United States. These people were particularly disappointed at China's unwillingness to cooperate on a number of vital issues like Iran, climate change, and North Korea; angry at China's alleged arrogance and assertiveness; and alarmed at what they perceived as the eroding status of the United States as a result of the increasing influence of a rising China.

In the meantime came the bizarre claim of the Obama administration to want to get "back to East Asia." Since this superpower has never left the Asia-Pacific, the "return" could only mean the determination of Washington to take substantial steps to reconsolidate its position in the region, a position that had been perceived to be greatly eroded owing to the negligence of the previous administration. These steps include redeploying the U.S. military in the region, making the Asia-Pacific now the most concentrated place of its sophisticated military assets abroad; strengthening old military alliances and seeking new security partners in Southeast Asia; enhancing its military presence in the form of conducting joint military exercises with local countries and port visits of its warships; and seeking other forms of bilateral and multilateral cooperation.

A Chinese soldier on exercises with Pakistan Army troops. Beijing has relied on nontraditional security missions to improve security ties with various key international partners. More robust China-U.S. cooperation in nontraditional security could help to ease anxieties in crucial but troubled regions, such as South and also Central Asia.

The "China threat" has been conspicuously used to justify these efforts. It has become almost an unwritten central theme that has run through all the recent dramas played out in both Northeast Asia and Southeast Asia.

In Northeast Asia, the *Cheonan* incident appeared like a God-given opportunity to the Americans, who seemed to want just such high tension in the region to justify American military presence and to arrest the centrifugal trends of its allies. In Southeast Asia, the Obama administration has noticeably been seeking to strengthen its position in the region by making use of China's territorial and maritime disputes with a number of ASEAN countries. In this regard, the State Department and Pentagon played a particularly active role in insinuating the "China threat" and portraying the United States as "the ultimate guarantor of regional peace and stability in South Asia."

U.S. initiatives in both domains seemed to have two goals. One was to emphasize that the United States was back and would act as the protector of all the other East Asian countries in the region who may have apprehensions about the uncertain impact on their security of the fast development of China. But most of all, they seemed also intended to be a message to Beijing that the United States would firmly respond to any challenges by a rising China.

The major flaw of this U.S. strategy, however, is that Washington seems to address a vital security issue with a major tool that was efficient in the Cold War but is evidently outmoded in the post–Cold War era. Times have changed. Most of the security issues in East Asia today are political and economic in nature. American military forces or security alliances would hardly seem relevant to their resolution.

Despite deep-seated mutual suspicion among states, East Asia is characterized by dynamics for sustained economic development, witnessing the fastest economic growth as well as global trade increase since the end of the Cold War. This economic development in East Asia has also become a driving force for the nations in the region to strengthen cooperation among themselves, to seek peaceful solutions of numerous regional disputes, and to strive for a new regional security architecture that would ensure the security interests of all the states, not only one state or a group of states. Against that backdrop, mutual interdependence and mutual constraint among nations in East Asia have become the hallmarks of the situation in the region. In this sense, East Asia is a region that sees the most evident development of a trend of multipolarization: no single power or a power group is able to dictate the security affairs in the region without taking into account the interests of other countries; all the countries are more determined to be treated as equal partners in the regional, as well as global, affairs that involve their interests; and even U.S. allies like Japan and South Korea no longer wish to bind themselves blindly to the U.S. war machine, although they continue to regard their respective alliances as the bedrock of their national security.

Under such circumstances, East Asia is now in the process of reshaping the balance of forces. It does not necessarily mean the decline of the absolute power of the United States, particularly in the military field. But the region has definitely seen the emergence of new economies, with rising roles in the political and security fields. China is just a case in point. The country reportedly became the second-largest economy last year, surpassing Japan in terms of the GDP. Just six years ago China's gross domestic product was about half of Japan's. As China is still a developing country, it has a lot of room to grow in the future. To imagine that the East Asian countries would be willing to join the United States in confronting China's rise is but wishful thinking.

Foreign Secretary Alberto Romulo of the Philippines, for example, explicitly stressed that "Southeast Asian nations don't need Washington's help in solving territorial disputes with China over the potentially resource-rich South China Sea" and that "negotiations should be strictly between the Association of Southeast Asian Nations (ASEAN) and China, without the U.S. or any other party involved." He refused to support the statement of Hillary Clinton hinting at greater U.S. involvement in the South China Sea.[3] Another illustrative example is that despite the fact that Vietnam showed some enthusiasm for strengthening its economic and defense ties with Washington, Hanoi has been out to make it clear that "Vietnam will never join a military alliance with the United States."[4]

II

Washington's unhappiness also seems to derive from misperceptions about China. Quite a number of myths play a very negative role in forging Washington's mind-set toward

China-U.S. relations. Misperception always gives rise to excessive fear, miscalculation, and overreaction.

Myth One: China Has Already Become a World Superpower

It is true China has achieved remarkable progress in terms of economic development over the past three decades, thanks to the opening to the outside and reform policy launched since 1978. For all these impressive figures, however, China is still a developing country, and the largest one in the world at that. Despite the fact China has become the second-largest economy in the world recently, the quality of its economic growth is yet to match its pace of expansion. In addition, China remains far behind many countries when per capita GDP is taken into account. In 2009, China reported a per capita GDP of $3,687, as compared to $37,800 for Japan and $46,436 for the United States. China ranked 103rd worldwide in terms of per capita GDP, according to the World Bank.[5] Thus, it is important to bear in mind that China's rise is more a process than a reality. As Deng Xiaoping once put it, China would have to make enormous efforts by generation upon generation to become a well-to-do country by the mid-twenty-first century.

Myth Two: China Is an Expansionist Power

China's numerous territorial and maritime disputes with its neighbors are often cited to showcase China's "expansionist" or "irredentist" ambition. Nothing indeed could wrong China more in that respect. If one examines each of these disputes closely, none was created by the People's Republic of China. They have all been left over by history. Moreover, since its founding the new China has been making consistent efforts to bring all these disputes to a peaceful solution. Not all of them were successful, as, the disputes having involved sovereignty and territorial integrity, each of the national governments concerned has found little room for compromise. China is no exception. That is why even military frictions or conflicts occurred between China and its neighbors, such as India and Vietnam, on a few occasions along the land or maritime borders. But even so, Beijing was always on the defensive, in each of these events, always showing great restraint to return to the status quo and working to stabilize the situation pending the final solution. Meanwhile, China has also succeeded in resolving many of the land-border disputes with almost all its neighbors, except with India, through peaceful negotiation in a spirit of mutual respect and mutual compromise. In many cases, it is Beijing, not the other sides, who made even greater concessions in order to clinch a deal. In consequence, China's territory has shrunk somewhat rather than expanded since 1949, when the People's Republic was founded.

In a more profound sense, China is in fact an inward-looking country. As Chinese leaders have often stated, the greatest challenges or threats to China's security come from within rather than from outside its boundaries. Given a most complex domestic environment, it would be no exaggeration to suggest that most of the time, energy, and interest of Chinese leaders has been focused before, and will be focused in the future, on domestic rather than international issues.

According to Zheng Bijian, one of the most prominent scholars in China, China has entered a critical, bottleneck period in its development. "China is now facing in particular five great challenges down the road: the shortage of energy resources; the degradation of its ecological environment; a series of issues as a result of the loss of economic and social balance during the course of development; massive natural disasters nationwide; and various international economic, political, scientific, cultural and military pressures as well as the existential and potential crises in the world China is confronted with." To meet all these challenges, and to ensure its sustained development, Zheng believes, China has no previous experience to learn from.

> China must act in a way fundamentally distinct from three types of approaches that rising world powers tried as they emerged in history: 1) the old Western powers accomplished their industrialization by relying on colonialist plunder of world resources in modern history; 2) Nazi Germany and militarist Japan sought to divide the world by unleashing wars in the first part of last century; 3) Soviet hegemony pursued a competition with another superpower in the scramble for spheres of influence during the Cold War. China can follow none of those formulas, and must define its own way of peaceful and civilized development characterized with seeking peace internationally and harmony at home.[6]

In short, what China has been trying to do is a grand economic and social experiment that is unprecedented in scale in human history. Not much time, indeed, has been left for China to harbor so-called expansionist ambitions. With regard to its foreign affairs, Beijing largely acted only to respond to what the other powers had done that was perceived to have implications for its security.

Myth Three: China Will Become More Bellicose When It Develops

Many Western pundits fear that China will become more aggressive when it finds its national interests expanding overseas, particularly when it requires precious energy and mineral resources to sustain its economic development. But this is also a misperception that largely derives from Western security culture. Based on their own experience of seeing the rise of one major power after another, always accompanied with the rising assertiveness of the newly rising power for more rights and prerogatives at the expense of other powers, people in the West simply do not understand why China will not follow the pattern. But the truth is perhaps just the opposite—that is, the more China develops, the more cooperative China will be as a responsible member of the international community.

China is keenly aware that it must rely on its own strength as well as on a more scientific mode of development to sustain its economic dynamics. If China were to follow the way of development in the West, by consuming energy in such an extravagant manner as we see in the United States and Europe today, even if all the world's energy were under the control of China, Beijing would still find it inadequate to meet its insatiable requirements. Obviously, China cannot follow that road. China must define a way to develop its own market by relying on its efforts and, moreover, endeavor to change its development mode, dramatically enhance the efficiency of energy consumption, and realize economic development based on the creation of green energy. To try to get a due share of the world market does constitute one solution. But that is only supplementary. In short, China must sustain its development in a more scientific way. Instead of becoming a cause of anarchic competition, energy is most likely to become an area of international cooperation.

A more fundamental reason for China to insist on cooperation is that its sustained development has already been imbedded in the health of the world economy, and its security within the security of the world. China sincerely wishes the United States to pull out of the economic recession as soon as possible, because the health of the U.S. economy is also in the best interests of China. Growing economic interdependence makes it futile for any major power, be it the United States or China, to resort to a confrontational approach in pursuit of narrowly defined national interests. That explains why China is strongly opposed to the shortsighted protectionist measures often seen in the developed countries, including the United States, in the name of protecting their national interests during the financial crisis and world recession.

China is in good faith in the hope of building up a long-term stable and peaceful international environment so as to concentrate on domestic development and develop cooperation at different levels. When international or regional disputes emerge, China hopes to solve them through peaceful means in a spirit of mutual respect, mutual benefit, equality, and mutual compromise. Military force is essential to defending the national interests of each nation. But it can only be employed as the last resort and must not be abused.

Myth Four: China Wants to Change the Rules of the Game

It is true that China is not a country satisfied with the existing political and economic world order. In China's conceptualization of a better world, there should be a new international order, which, based on sincere respect for the purpose and principles of the United Nations Charter, sees the greater democratization in international affairs and the assurance of peace and development of all nations. China thus does wish to see the modification of the existing world order to a certain extent in order to realize a more balanced world structure, as well as a more just and fair world order.

But the more important question is what China sees as the best approach to achieving that goal. The following are the highlights of China's position. First, China hopes to build up the new world order by reform, through the concerted efforts of all nations and in an evolutionary way. Reform means retaining the best part of the old systems while introducing new elements. Second, China holds that a new world order is possible only through the best understanding and cooperation between the developed and developing countries. It is feasible only when it can take into account the interests of all nations. Thus, changing the rules of game is going to be a long process, the process of coordinating and accommodating various interests in the world.

Third, China believes that the two most influential powers in the world, China and the United States, need not come into conflict on the issue. On the contrary, they share many common interests in seeing the emergence of such a new world order and in working together in this long process. The close consultations between the two countries during the debate concerning United Nations reform and the creation of the Group of Twenty (G-20) and current efforts for the restructuring of the world financial monetary and regulatory mechanisms are just a few good examples among many others to show that China and the United States have actually already cooperated on this issue. Fourth, in East Asia, China has consistently expressed its wish to see a change of the game to promote greater peace and stability. The role of the U.S.-led military alliance in the region, for example, has never been viewed by China as a positive and stabilizing factor. However, China has also made it clear that since the American-led military alliances are all bilateral in nature, China would respect the decision of the national governments concerned if they continue to think the alliance is necessary for them, as long as no country wants to use the alliance for military interference in China's internal affairs, thereby undermining China's security interests.

Misgivings and mistrust do emerge over the rules of game. In China's view, they come mainly from mixed feelings in Washington—while acknowledging the inevitability of the emergence of a new world structure and the efforts of all nations to adapt to the new situation, the United States seems to continue to harbor an unrealistic wish not to lose its dominance over the world and a fear that the rising China would become potentially the greatest challenge to its world hegemony. Much, therefore, depends on perceptions regarding the need to change the game and an effective approach to accomplish this change.

III

While the two countries are constrained in the traditional security field, nontraditional security cooperation between China and the United States can help facilitate better understanding, foster common interests, and promote mutual confidence and trust. At the very least, this concept can serve as useful ballast for the ship of the bilateral relationship, for the stabilization of the ship in rough seas.

China's President Hu Jintao offers condolences to a relative of a Chinese peacekeeper killed by the massive earthquake in Haiti. Other Chinese peacekeeping missions have also suffered fatalities, such as the mission in Lebanon.

Obviously, all these myths in Washington will not disappear in the foreseeable future. They will likely continue to feed American disquiet and even alarm over China and generate a poisonous atmosphere in the evolution of China-U.S. relations. But one need not be overly pessimistic. This bilateral relationship has never seen a linear pattern. While constrained in the traditional security fields, the two countries continue to see a growing number of overlapping interests in their cooperation in the nontraditional security fields.

Incentives for cooperation in the field of nontraditional security have become even more pronounced, for three reasons. One is that the post–Cold War years have seen a noticeable rise of nontraditional security threats, which have not only brought devastating effects impacting the security of individual nations, as shown by the 9/11 terrorist attacks on the United States, but become the major cause of regional, as well as international, instability, violence, and turmoil. They have become the common scourge in the international community. Secondly, as nontraditional security threats are often transnational or transregional, no country alone can effectively cope with them. Thus, China and the United States together confront a long list of issues like terrorism, proliferation of weapons of mass destruction, illicit drugs, HIV/AIDS, piracy, illegal migration, environmental security, economic security, food security, information security, and energy, among many others, that call on the two countries to work together. This trend will not abate even when the two capitals continue to be burdened with heavy misgivings about each other. Last but not least, when the two countries are seriously constrained in the traditional security field, enhancing nontraditional security cooperation could facilitate better understanding of the two sides, foster common interests, and promote mutual confidence and trust.

The first area of feasible cooperation concerns many vital issues that are closely related to the economic security of the two countries. The two sides have an ever-stronger interest in expanding cooperation in this respect. This common understanding was also reflected in the China-U.S. joint statement signed in November 2009. The document devoted much attention to defining areas of bilateral economic and trade cooperation. Cooperation essentially requires that the two countries continue to advance China-U.S. economic and trade ties, strengthen macroeconomic policy coordination and their cooperation in the framework of the G-20 to push for further recovery in the world economy, and work together to better address such issues as climate change, energy security, food security, and technology cooperation.

The second area of cooperation includes issues related to political as well as social security and stability. Antiterrorism, nonproliferation, and the fight against ethnic separatism and religious extremism belong to the field of political security, while issues like illicit drugs, HIV/AIDS, illegal migration, environmental security, and food security belong to the realm of human security. In both fields, China and the United States need to support each other, as these types of threats know no boundaries or limitations in terms of the cause of problems and their disastrous effects. What happens in New York today could happen in London, Moscow, or Beijing or any other city tomorrow. Among all these issues, how to wind down the war in Afghanistan and ensure sustained stability based on the efficient governance by the Afghan government could be crucial to the success of the international effort in combating terrorism. Equally important, seeking solutions to both the Iran and North Korea nuclear crises, in ways acceptable to all the parties concerned, would also be essential to strengthening the nonproliferation regime. China and the United States continue to share the same fundamental objective on both accounts.

The third area that is particularly pertinent, and perhaps carries some practical urgency for China-U.S. cooperation, is maritime security. As China sees an increasing stake in the oceans, its interests in cooperation with the United States are mounting. One important driver for better communication and cooperation in the maritime field between China and the United States is the fact that the two sides share the belief that a better mechanism to ensure good governance on the oceans would be in their best interests. The oceans have long seen growing complexity owing to the increasing interest in maritime issues among the national priorities among many powers, the buildup of naval capabilities, the prospect of competition for maritime resources, and the rise of piracy, among other reasons. As a result, both China and the United States would like to see the prevention of the expansion of ungoverned maritime space, on one hand, and of a looming maritime arms competition, on the other. China's decision in 2008 to join the counterpiracy efforts off the Horn of Africa is indicative of Beijing's willingness to participate in the international cooperation in the maintenance of maritime peace and stability. So far, cooperation in that field has been going well. In the meantime, however, competition among major powers in the maritime domain seems also to be rising, and that trend has already produced a good deal of uncertainty.

There are, of course, risks in cooperating in nontraditional security. It could easily become hostage to the deep-seated suspicion between the two countries, as demonstrated in the traditional security field. After all, nontraditional security issues tend to crop up in the traditional security context, one way or the other. Whether Washington considers Beijing a truly strategic partner or as a potential threat, for example, would be decisive as to the extent to which China-U.S. cooperation in the nontraditional security cooperation could develop in the future.

As in the traditional security field, it is imperative that cooperation in nontraditional security be conducted in a spirit of mutual respect and mutual benefit, and on an equal footing. Often the Chinese feel frustrated at the high-handed manner expressed by Washington, as if cooperation simply means that China should do as the United States dictates. Otherwise, China is invariably labeled "irresponsible" or "arrogant." This attitude is particularly offensive when the two sides have differences on the appropriate approach to a common objective. Sanctions against Iran are a case in point. China did not think extra sanctions beyond the request of the UN Security Council were conducive to the eventual solution of the nuclear crisis. However, Washington thought differently and then shoveled onto China all responsibility for the lack of progress on this issue.

The Chinese sometimes also resent the double standards in bilateral cooperation with the United States in the nontraditional security arena. When the American administration refused to repatriate those terrorists of Chinese Uighur ethnic nationality captured in Afghanistan on the grounds that they could hardly be looked on as terrorists by the U.S. standard, it can be imagined how the Chinese people felt about it. Many, in their irrational emotion, even questioned the value for China of continuing to cooperate with the "ungrateful and treacherous Americans" in that respect. Countries must respect each other in their interactions.

IV

The Obama administration is running the risk of making a mess of its China policy. It has unnecessarily pushed the bilateral relations to a new level of tension, dimming the prospect of cooperating with Beijing on many vital security issues. It is argued that all this came out of the deep-seated mistrust between the two powers. That certainly makes some sense. But mistrust is only a symptom; behind it there seems a more fundamental cause for the misplaced China policy in Washington, driven by a poor appreciation in the United States of how fast the world is changing, by the inertia of stereotypical thinking developed in the Cold War, and by the excessive apprehension about a rising China as the major potential threat.

The key test to the United States with respect to the future of China-U.S. relations, therefore, is whether Washington is able to come to terms with the development of the world situation, including the rise of China. That requires a new vision, accepting that China's development is inevitable and that the rise of China is not necessarily detrimental to the core interests of the United States. On the contrary, a rising China could offer a unique opportunity to develop an overall, comprehensive partnership with Beijing, a great help to the United States in coping with current predicaments.

This is chiefly because China wants to be a friend and not an adversary of the United States. If history is any guide, the course of China-U.S. relations over the past half-century or more should lead to three important conclusions: first, China and the United States both gain from peaceful coexistence and lose from conflicts; second, mutual interest serves as the bedrock of our cooperation; and third, China-U.S. cooperation is conducive to stability in the Asia-Pacific region, as well as to peace and development in the world. Based on this understanding, the Chinese government has consistently held the view that "to strengthen China-U.S. cooperation is not only a mutual need but also a responsibility, which the two countries shoulder in the interest of world peace and development. In case of differences and contradictions, both sides should keep cool and be sensible, and try to increase communications, reduce mistrust and seek common ground while shelving differences with a view to properly handling these differences and contradictions."[7]

This does not suggest, of course, that the United States has the sole responsibility for the health of China-U.S. relations. The recent frictions between the two countries seem revealing regarding excessive responses from Beijing also. To cut off all military relations, including dialogues, as a response to recent American policies that seriously undermine China's core interests is understandable. But to use it as a means of retaliation against U.S. actions is hardly a wise strategy, because at the end of the day, keeping communication smooth is an essential part of the efforts of both countries to maintain working relations and therefore is in the interests of both sides.

More worrisome is the emergence in China of a school of thought that, rather like that of neoconservatives in the United States, seems to seek only confrontation with the other side. These people, amusingly, hold views so similar to those of their conservative counterparts in Washington that I sometimes even suspect that they may have stolen these American views. Like their American counterparts, they bemoan the grave situation the country is faced with—in China's case, as a result of the U.S. encirclement in the Asia-Pacific. They argue that since China has already become a world power, China should strive to be "second to none" and that now is the time to show its military muscles, not least because of the need to protect ever increasing overseas national interests. They also hold that China, in particular, should be firm with respect to the provocations from the superpower by staging a tit-for-tat struggle. These views by no means represent the views of the Chinese government. They are not even the mainstream views of the Chinese public. They, however, have their own impact in confusing the minds of average Chinese citizens, as well as of people abroad.

Realizing the dream of an enduring China-U.S. partnership will require concerted efforts from both sides.

Notes

1. "China-US Joint Statement," *Ministry of Foreign Affairs,* 17 November 2009, www.fmprc.gov.cn/.
2. Ibid.
3. "Washington Not Needed in South China Sea Issue: Manila Source," *Global Times,* 10 August 2010, world.globaltimes.cn/.
4. "Vietnam, China Step Up Defense Ties," *Voice of Vietnam,* 11 August 2010, english.vovnews.vn/.
5. See Wang Xiaotian and Li Xiang, "China Overtakes Japan in Economic Prowess," *China Daily,* 17 August 2010.
6. Zheng Bijian, "Peaceful Development and the Review and Prospect of the Relations across the Taiwan Straits" (keynote speech, "Academic Conference on the Sixtieth Anniversary of the Relations across the Taiwan Straits," Taipei, 13 November 2009). The Chinese version of the speech is available at *Study Times,* theory.people.com.cn/. The lines quoted were translated by the present author.
7. See Wen Jiabao, "Working Together to Write a New Chapter in China-US Relations" (speech by the premier of China's State Council at dinner hosted by nine American organizations during his visit to the United States, 9 December 2003), available at www.fmprc.gov.cn/.

China's Maritime Reemergence and U.S.-China Naval Cooperation in the NTS Domain

Kristen Gunness

The past decade has heralded significant changes in the maritime realm. Some of the most prominent of these changes have been driven by the reemergence of China as a full-fledged participant in the international order—economically, politically, diplomatically, and in security affairs. As China adjusts to its role as a power with widespread global interests, it must also come to grips with how to protect those interests. China's reemergence and larger role in world affairs thus have been the primary impetus behind the Chinese People's Liberation Army's (PLA's) crosscutting military modernization program and behind Hu Jintao's 2004 announcement of the New Historic Missions, which ordered the PLA to develop the capabilities necessary to protect China's increasingly global interests.[1]

These are the capabilities that we see the PLA and the PLA Navy put to use today in nontraditional security operations. Recent examples of these new capabilities include China's first noncombatant evacuation operation (NEO), conducted in Libya in February 2011, wherein the PLAN dispatched a *Xuzhou* missile frigate to evacuate Chinese citizens; PLA disaster-relief teams who were ready to come to Japan's aid after the March 2011 tsunami; deployment of the PLAN's new hospital ship, *Daishandao* (Peace Ark), to countries in the Asia-Pacific region and farther abroad; and, of course, the continuing counterpiracy missions off the coast of Somalia.

These missions represent the first steps onto what is undoubtedly a critical path toward Chinese ability to protect its economic and security interests around the globe and to become a preeminent regional power, with increasing global presence. Many of the capabilities the PLA is developing for these nontraditional security missions are maritime-related or have naval components, providing increased potential for U.S.-China naval cooperation in NTS areas.

This paper discusses the opportunities for U.S.-China naval cooperation in NTS areas. First, it examines two drivers of change in the maritime domain attendant on China's reemergence as a major power. Second, the paper discusses the current state of U.S.-China cooperation in the maritime domain. Third, it analyzes future prospects for cooperation between the two navies in the NTS domain.

China's Reemergence and Two Drivers of Change in the Maritime Domain

There are at least two key realities of China's reemergence that are drivers of change in the maritime domain and that have implications for how the U.S. and Chinese navies will approach and pursue cooperation in the future.

Reality One: China today, more than ever before, has global economic interests that depend on the stability and security of the maritime domain. The stability and security of the maritime commons are increasingly important for China as its economic interests become more global. China's dependence on the oceans is quite tangible:

- Recent Chinese statistics published in the 2010 *China's Ocean Development Report* state that in 2008 ocean commerce represented 9.87 percent of China's gross domestic product, valued at approximately $450 billion. About 85 percent of China's international trade uses shipping lanes.[2]

- China is now the world's second-largest economy, and some statistics state that by 2020, the value of its maritime commerce will exceed a trillion dollars a year.

- According to the International Energy Agency, China will have to rely on imports for 79 percent of its oil needs by 2030.[3] Eighty-five percent of these oil imports, from both the Middle East and Africa, flow through the Straits of Malacca before heading into the South China Sea, amplifying the strategic importance of this major choke point for China's economy.[4]

In addition, China's coastline is eighteen thousand kilometers long; the nation claims over four million square miles of sea area, operates over 1,400 harbors, and has a merchant marine of about 1,800 ships. Also, China has six of the world's top ten ports by cargo.[5] This is just what the PLA Navy must protect at home—never mind protecting the nation's interests abroad.

As China becomes more dependent on ocean-borne trade, its maritime concerns and perceptions of security threats, particularly in the nontraditional security arena, have become more complex. Some of these concerns include the following:

- Energy insecurity, as China's dependence on foreign energy sources and its inability to secure its sea-lanes leave it vulnerable. Recently, this concern has led to increased tensions in the South China Sea as China attempts to enforce territorial claims that would give it access to natural resources in the area.

- Piracy that threatens China's merchant fleet, in the South China Sea, in the Straits of Malacca, and most recently in the Horn of Africa.

- Nonstate actors and terrorist organizations, which could disrupt key shipping lanes and the maritime flow of commerce.

A Dual-Track Approach

China has so far responded to these concerns with a dual-track approach—building legal foundations for access, and rapid military modernization. On the legal front, China has attempted to build the foundations in international law necessary to ensure its access to critical areas of the high seas. This includes trying to garner support for its interpretation of the United Nations Convention on the Law of the Sea (UNCLOS), one differing from that of the majority of coastal states.

Under its interpretation of UNCLOS, China primarily objects to the conduct of military research activities in its EEZ, insisting that these activities are unlawful and that they constitute abuses of freedom of navigation.[6] Tensions between the United States and China over the EEZ issue rose in March 2009 when USNS *Impeccable,* an unarmed military research ship operating in the South China Sea, was harassed by Chinese fishing vessels. Since then, safety at sea has been a top priority for the U.S. Navy, and the U.S. and Chinese navies have held discussions on this topic. However, the larger issue of access to the maritime commons remains. In particular, right of access to EEZs and what activities one is permitted to undertake in those waters remain points of contentious debate between the United States and China.

Developing New Maritime Capabilities. On the military modernization front, China is attempting to address its maritime security concerns by building up the PLA/PLAN's capabilities, resulting in increased ability to project force; the ability to conduct more complex missions outside China's littoral waters;[7] and increased ability to participate in what the PLA has labeled as "military operations other than war" (MOOTW).[8]

The most obvious manifestation of this is the PLA Navy's participation in the multinational counterpiracy operations in the Gulf of Aden. Since December 2008, the PLAN has dispatched naval escort task forces to that region. These missions represent numerous "firsts" for the PLAN. To name a few: it is the first time PLAN ships have conducted operations in waters other than Chinese littoral waters; the first time the PLAN has operated forces over a long period of time away from home port; and the first time the PLAN has had to operate for an extended period of time as part of a multinational effort.[9] So far the PLAN has shown a remarkable ability to learn and adapt quickly, and the task forces have successfully executed their missions. All indications are that the Chinese navy will continue to support the counterpiracy operations in the Gulf of Aden for the foreseeable future.

As China's expanding regional and global interests create broader requirements for military capabilities, the PLA and PLAN will increasingly be called on to prepare for and take part in activities such as the counterpiracy missions, or other MOOTW activities. For China's leadership, involvement in such activities enhances the country's image as a

China's hospital ship, Peace Ark, *passes close to a Chinese destroyer in the Indian Ocean. China's improving capabilities for humanitarian aid and disaster relief suggest the possibility of closer coordination with the U.S. Navy in this area. Then-CNO Admiral Gary Roughead visited* Peace Ark *in 2009 and promoted professional exchanges between the U.S. and Chinese naval medical establishments.*

constructive player in global security affairs, and for the PLA these activities offer valuable operational experience that enhance its ability to conduct the full range of operations. In addition, given China's growing stake in the security of the maritime commons, it is not far-fetched to think that another mission the Chinese leadership might envision for the PLA in the future would be the protection of key sea lines of communications (SLOCs) to safeguard China's maritime energy and trade routes if necessary.

Reality Two: China is now proactively shaping the international security environment, not merely reacting to it. China has reemerged as a full participant in the larger international order after almost two centuries. As a result, the PRC is engaging internationally on every front—politically, economically, diplomatically, and in security affairs.

China is using all of the elements of national power to shape proactively the regional and international security environment. This includes being a more active participant in international and regional organizations, such as the Six-Party Talks and the Shanghai Cooperation Organization. It includes using its economic clout to collect resources overseas and invest in other countries' markets. Finally, it includes conducting military diplomacy and, significantly, using the PLA as an operational asset to support China's larger national objectives.

Building "Soft Power" Capabilities

In the maritime domain, China is shaping regional perceptions and promoting its "peaceful rise" by building up soft-power capabilities. As a growing regional power,

China clearly wants both to assuage concerns about how it will use its capabilities and to play a larger role in regional affairs befitting a regional power. In particular, the PLA/PLAN is strengthening its ability to respond to relief after natural disasters and humanitarian crises.

This effort began in earnest after the 2004 Indian Ocean tsunami, where the PLA's presence was either lacking or conspicuously limited in the disaster-relief efforts, especially in comparison to the U.S. military.[10] Since then, the PLA has participated in more HA/DR efforts beyond the domestic natural disasters it has already supported, such as the 2008 Sichuan earthquake. For example, the PLA had a significant presence in the earthquakes in Pakistan and Haiti, and it was ready to offer assistance in the Japan tsunami disaster. The PLAN has followed suit, recently commissioning its new hospital ship, the two-thousand-ton, five-hundred-bed *Daishandao,* which first deployed in October 2009 and has since made several deployments as far abroad as Africa and, most recently, even to the Caribbean.[11]

In addition to the hospital ship, the PLAN has taken some steps to develop its search-and-rescue capabilities. According to the 2008 white paper on China's national defense, China has conducted joint maritime search and rescue training exercises (SAREXes) with Australia and New Zealand in the Tasman Sea.[12] In addition, in 2006 the U.S. and Chinese navies conducted a search-and-rescue exercise, in conjunction with a port visit by the PLAN to San Diego.

Increased Power Projection

China is also proactively shaping regional perceptions by building up its power-projection capability through its aircraft carrier program, which could potentially deploy the nation's first aircraft carriers in the coming years. While this development, in and of itself, is not unexpected, given China's rising status as a regional power, it has compounded the uncertainty of other countries in the region as to China's intentions. Chinese leaders seem well aware of this: in November 2008 the director of the Foreign Affairs Office in the Ministry of National Defense, Maj. Gen. Qian Lihua, said that "having an aircraft carrier is the dream of any great military power," and "the question is not whether you have an aircraft carrier, but what you do with your aircraft carrier."[13]

Analysts still maintain that China has a long way to go before it can successfully operate an aircraft carrier. However, the idea that the PRC is building such a maritime capability is already shaping perceptions of China's role in the region, not just because it will increase China's ability to get to more places and project power farther afield but also because it advances the perception of a reemergent China that is a major participant in regional and global security affairs.

Chinese nationals line up to evacuate from the intensifying civil war in Libya in February 2011. The Chinese navy sent a frigate to monitor the evacuation, which also relied heavily on chartered civilian vessels such as the one shown here. As a global power, Beijing will likely be drawn more frequently into complex contingencies around the world. This trend underscores the importance of nontraditional security for future Chinese foreign and defense policy.

In sum, these realities indicate that as China's interests become global, the reasons for China to care about the stability and security of the maritime commons have increased. Also, China is taking a much more proactive approach to shaping the security environment around it, including the development of more soft power and power projection in the maritime domain. In addition, China is building capabilities that will enable it to be a greater participant in nontraditional security areas—including humanitarian disaster relief and multinational operations like the Horn of Africa counterpiracy mission.

Implications of These Realities

What are the implications of these realities, and how are they significant to the future of U.S.-China naval cooperation?

First, China will continue to invest in the PLAN and develop the capabilities necessary to protect its interests abroad. Given that China is dependent on a stable and secure maritime environment in order to safeguard its economic growth, one can attribute at least some of China's investment in its navy as a sign that it is uncomfortable with continuing to depend solely on the United States to provide this security. Thus, as we look to the future and ask how China will pursue its national interests, we can expect to see a desire to establish self-reliance when it comes to such issues as ensuring ability to gain and maintain access to energy resources, protecting key SLOCs, and ensuring maritime security and unfettered shipping.

Second, as the PLA goes farther abroad, there will be more interaction between the U.S. and Chinese navies. The counterpiracy missions are likely the first of many the PLAN will conduct outside China's littoral waters. The PLAN's new hospital ship will also put American and Chinese naval forces in contact with each other should a natural disaster occur. Also, of course, as the PLAN increases its operational tempo around the Asia-Pacific region—particularly in the East China Sea, the South China Sea, and the Yellow Sea—the U.S. and Chinese navies will encounter each other more. The goal is to ensure that these interactions occur professionally and safely and that they are viewed as opportunities for the two navies to learn from each other.

Of course, there also will be an increase in unplanned interactions in unexpected places around the globe. For example, as access to the arctic becomes more viable, it is conceivable that American and Chinese maritime forces might find themselves encountering each other more often in that part of the world.

Third, China's maritime reemergence will continue to result in a mixture of areas of cooperation and contention. In many areas, China is being a constructive participant in resolving international maritime security issues, and this is greatly welcomed by the U.S. Navy. The counterpiracy missions and the PLAN's participation in the Shared Awareness and Deconfliction (SHADE) group are examples of constructive cooperation between the navies of the world, ones in which China is playing a significant role. In some areas, however, there has been tension as China challenges existing maritime norms—the tension over lawful military activities in exclusive economic zones is an example of this, as is increased tension in the South China Sea. It is likely that this dynamic of cooperation and contention will always exist, and the more the United States and China can maintain an open dialogue—at high levels as well as with lower-level cooperative efforts—the better we will be able to make our way through the rough patches.

Fourth, the reasons to cooperate are increasing. The realities discussed above suggest that the United States and China have more reasons than ever before to cooperate in the maritime domain. China's reemergence, its increased reliance on the maritime commons, and its greater stake in ensuring their stability and security provide a broader foundation on which our navies can cooperate than existed in the past. Additionally, while some aspects of China's naval modernization have caused concern for the United States, the PLA is developing capabilities that will allow it to cooperate better with U.S. forces in other regions around the globe, which is in both nations' interests.

The New Maritime Strategy and U.S.-China Naval Cooperation

In 2007, the maritime forces (Navy, Marine Corps, and Coast Guard) of the United States published a unified maritime strategy, "A Cooperative Strategy for 21st Century Seapower." This new strategy lays the groundwork for future naval cooperation in NTS areas.

The maritime strategy is about security, stability, and sea power. It rests on three key principles:

- Securing the United States from direct attack
- Securing strategic access and retaining global freedom of action
- Strengthening existing and emerging alliances and partnerships and establishing favorable security conditions.

The maritime strategy emphasizes that the prevention of war is as important as winning war. It thus focuses on *collective security*—maritime forces will be employed to build confidence and trust among nations through efforts that focus on common threats and mutual interests in an open, multipolar world. It elevates humanitarian assistance and disaster relief to core elements of maritime power; whereas in the past U.S. maritime forces have participated in these efforts, now they will integrate them into their planning processes. This strategy reaffirms the need for regionally concentrated, forward-deployed combat power while also taking a "global view" and placing a new emphasis on globally distributed, mission-tailored maritime forces.

So what does this mean for U.S.-China naval cooperation? The new maritime strategy contains a variety of elements that provide a basis for enhanced maritime cooperation with China. First, the emphasis on conflict prevention is a shared interest, one that both sides can agree on. Second, the strategy's objective of securing the global maritime commons is highly compatible with China's strategic interests as a power with global economic and security interests, as discussed above. Third, the new emphasis on humanitarian operations, especially, offers opportunities for bilateral cooperation to build mutual trust without participating in activities that Beijing may deem objectionable.

Current U.S.-China Cooperative Maritime Security Efforts

The United States and China are already cooperating on a number of maritime security activities, many of which are in the NTS domain. They include:

- *Global Maritime Partnership (GMP):* China has been invited to cooperate more broadly with the U.S. Navy under the framework of the Global Maritime Partnership, as set forth in the new maritime strategy. The GMP, also known as the "Thousand-Ship Navy," was proposed by Adm. Michael Mullen, then Chief of Naval Operations.

The vision was to create a "partnership" of like-minded countries to combat common threats at sea. Under this vision, nations participating in the GMP program seek opportunities to assist one another in using the sea for lawful purposes and legitimate commerce, while limiting its use by those who threaten national, regional, or global security.[14]

- *PLAN doctors on board USNS* Comfort: In June 2009, four PLAN doctors visited USNS *Comfort* (T-AH 20), one of the U.S. Navy's hospital ships, for a week to observe medical procedures. This was the first time such an exchange of medical personnel had occurred between the two navies.

- *Counterpiracy and SHADE*: China's counterpiracy efforts have been welcomed by the United States and the other international participants. The PLAN recently deployed yet another task force to the region. So far, cooperation between the U.S. Navy and the PLAN has been limited, but it has been happening. In particular, we have seen some notable cooperation on ship-to-ship communications between the United States and China in the Gulf of Aden, particularly in sharing relevant intelligence. The Shared Awareness and Deconfliction group, based in Bahrain, provides a working-level opportunity for the forty-plus navies participating in the counterpiracy operations off the Horn of Africa to come together to share information and deconflict their efforts. Reflecting China's willingness to take a larger role in multinational counterpiracy operations, in January 2010 the PRC committed itself to supply one warship to the Horn of Africa to patrol a sixty-nautical-mile stretch along the Internationally Recommended Transit Corridor (IRTC). This commitment makes China eligible to lead the coalition, the chairmanship of which is rotated every three to four months.[15] Until recently, China has mainly escorted its own merchant ships and has not taken part in the larger coalition.

- *MMCA:* The Military Maritime Consultative Agreement was established in 1998. The agreement provides for operator-level exchanges to discuss issues of maritime safety and communication, as well as for expanding cooperation in areas such as search and rescue and humanitarian assistance. It provides a forum to discuss issues over international maritime regulations and to develop a common understanding of operating procedures when encounters between American and Chinese naval forces occur. It is the only "official" venue for dialogue between the U.S. Navy and the PLAN.

- *Coast guard cooperation:* The U.S. Coast Guard has established a working relationship with its Chinese counterparts. In May 2006, the cutter *Sequoia* became the first U.S. cutter to visit China. In August 2007, USCGC *Boutwell* continued these exchanges with a visit to Shanghai during the North Pacific Coast Guard Forum, East Asia's only maritime security organization, in which China and the United States both played substantive roles.

- *The Container Security Initiative (CSI):* In 2002, China joined the Container Security Initiative, which aims to safeguard the global maritime trading system from terrorism. So far, China's participation has been limited to the ports of Shanghai and Shenzhen.

The Future of U.S.-China Naval Cooperation in Nontraditional Security Areas

Of course, it is difficult to discuss the future of U.S.-China naval cooperation without first addressing the elephant in the room. That elephant is the reality that U.S.-China naval cooperation—and indeed the whole military-to-military relationship—is a hostage to the larger bilateral political relationship, and that imposes limits on what the two navies can do cooperatively at any given time. The on-again, off-again dynamic of the U.S.-China military-to-military relationship, which is often "shut down" following American decisions to move forward with arms sales to Taiwan, illustrates this dilemma. Additionally, renewed tensions in the South China Sea have the potential to derail cooperative efforts, as U.S. and Chinese naval forces operating in the region must adhere to the political realities that the bilateral relationship faces as a result of rising tensions and competing interests.

On the other hand, it is precisely because such tensions exist that we should take advantage of the opportunity to cooperate when and where we can, in the hope that even small cooperative efforts can help manage tensions, create mutual understanding, and avert larger crises. As discussed above, the expansion of Chinese interests and capabilities creates, possibly for the first time, the basis for real cooperation. This is particularly true for cooperation in the NTS realm.

Despite the constraints, U.S. and Chinese naval forces are in a unique position to cooperate, in that there are many areas where our navies are already working together and where they will continue to work together. For example, U.S. Navy–PLAN cooperation in the counterpiracy operations off the coast of Somalia will not cease because of bilateral political issues. The move by China to take greater part in the multinational counterpiracy efforts by joining SHADE is welcomed by all. The deployment of the PLAN's hospital ship will undoubtedly create more opportunity for exchanges like the one aboard USNS *Comfort*. Also, as Chinese citizens live abroad in greater numbers, opportunities exist for our two navies to cooperate on future NEOs should the need arise.

In April 2009 Adm. Gary Roughead, then Chief of Naval Operations, met with Adm. Wu Shengli, commander of the PLAN, to discuss specific opportunities for cooperation in the maritime domain. In October 2009 then–secretary of defense Robert Gates and Gen. Xu Caihou agreed on concrete and practical measures to work on in the years ahead (dubbed the "Seven Points of Consensus"), and in July 2011 Admiral Mullen, then chairman of the Joint Chiefs of Staff, reiterated U.S. desire for cooperation with China.

Ultimately, the overarching long-term goals of U.S.-China navy-to-navy cooperation should be to help build cooperative capacity, foster institutional understanding, and develop common views on the international security environment and related security challenges. All of the initiatives listed above support these overall goals.

As the U.S. and Chinese navies look to the future, we should pay attention to positioning ourselves better to be able to seize cooperative opportunities when they arise. This means continuing to maintain an open dialogue when and where we can, including in the MMCA and in "track two" (informal and working-level) venues, to enhance mutual understanding and discuss differences. This type of ongoing interaction and dialogue, as demonstrated by this volume itself, will pave the way for future cooperative efforts in the maritime domain.

Notes

1. Daniel Hartnett, *Towards a Globally Focused Chinese Military: The Historic Missions of the Chinese Armed Forces* (Alexandria, Va.: Center for Naval Analyses, June 2008).
2. State Oceanic Administration, Ocean Development Strategy Research Study Group, *China's Ocean Development Report* (Beijing: Maritime Publishing House, 2010), p. 227.
3. Chris V. Nicholson, "China's Energy Industry Pushes into Developed Markets," *Dealbook*, 14 March 2011, dealbook.nytimes.com/.
4. For information on import and export statistics, see "Statistics: International Trade Statistics 2009," *World Trade Organization,* 2012, under "Trade by Region," www.wto.org/.
5. *Containerisation International Yearbook 2009* (London: Institute of Shipping Economics and Logistics, 2009; repr. New Orleans, La.: U.S. Army Corps of Engineers, Waterborne Commerce Statistics Center).
6. See Peter A. Dutton, "Charting a Course: U.S.-China Cooperation at Sea," *China Security* 5, no. 1 (Winter 2009), pp. 11–26.
7. In China's 2006 defense white paper, "China's National Defense in 2006," *People's Daily,* english.people.com.cn/whitepaper/defense2006/defense2006.html, China's government listed the gradual expansion of the PLA Navy's strategic depth as a national goal. It asserts, "The Navy aims at gradual extension of the strategic depth for offshore defensive operations and enhancing its capabilities in integrated maritime operations and nuclear counter attacks."
8. China's 2008 defense white paper listed the development of capabilities necessary to conduct "military operations other than war" as a focus for the PLA. These types of operations include counterterrorism, participation in UN peacekeeping, noncombatant evacuation, emergency disaster relief, international humanitarian assistance, and counterpiracy patrols.
9. Bud Cole, "China's Military and Security Activities Abroad"(testimony before the U.S.-China Economic and Security Review Commission, 4 March 2009, Washington, D.C.), available at www.uscc.gov/hearings/2009hearings/written_testimonies/09_03_04_wrts/09_03_04_cole_statement.pdf.
10. Drew Thompson, "Tsunami Relief Reflects China's Regional Aspirations," *China Brief* 5, no. 2 (January 2005).
11. "Peace Ark Hospital Ship Sets Out for Long-Distance Rounds-Making Mission," Xinhua, 21 October 2009, eng.mod.gov.cn/; PRC, *China's National Defense in 2010* (Beijing: Information Officer of the State Council, 2010), app. I, "Military Exchanges with Other Countries," available at news.xinhuanet.com/english2010/china/2011-03/31/c_13806851.htm.

12. PRC, *China's National Defense in 2008* (Beijing: Information Officer of the State Council, 2008), available at www.china.org.cn/government/central_government/2009-01/20/content_17155577.htm.

13. "China Has Aircraft Carrier Hopes," *BBC News*, 17 November 2008, news.bbc.co.uk/.

14. "'Global Maritime Partnership' Gaining Steam at Home and with International Navies," *Defense Daily*, 25 October 2006.

15. "Press Conference on Work of Contact Group on Piracy off Somali Coast," *United Nations*, 28 January 2010, www.un.org/; "Navies Agree on Set Areas for Somali Patrols," *China Daily*, 3 February 2010, www.chinadaily.com.cn/.

Abbreviations and Definitions

A
- **APEC** — Asia-Pacific Economic Cooperation
- **ASEAN** — Association of Southeast Asian Nations
- **ASW** — antisubmarine warfare
- **AU** — African Union

C
- **C4ISR** — command, control, communications, computer, intelligence, surveillance, and reconnaissance
- **CCP** — Chinese Communist Party
- **CIVPOL** — UN civilian police
- **CMATS** — Certain Maritime Arrangements in the Timor Sea
- **CMC** — Central Military Commission
- **CNAS** — Center for a New American Security
- **CPCTC** — China Peacekeeping CIVPOL Training Center
- **CSI** — Container Security Initiative
- **CTF** — Combined Task Force

D
- **DASD** — Deputy Assistant Secretary of Defense
- **DoD** — Department of Defense [U.S.]

E
- **EEZ** — exclusive economic zone
- **EU** — European Union

F
- **FOCAC** — Forum on China and Africa Cooperation

G
- **G-20** — Group of Twenty
- **GDP** — gross domestic product
- **GMP** — Global Maritime Partnership

	GoTL	government of Timor-Leste
	GPOI	Global Peace Operations Initiative
	GPS	Global Positioning System
	GSD	General Staff Department
H	**HA**	humanitarian assistance
	HA/DR	humanitarian assistance/disaster relief
	HIV/AIDS	human immunodeficiency virus/acquired immune deficiency syndrome
I	**IHA**	international humanitarian assistance
	INTERFET	International Force for East Timor
	IRTC	Internationally Recommended Transit Corridor
	ISF	International Stabilization Force [East Timor]
	IW	indication and warning
K	**KFOR**	Kosovo Force
L	**LHA**	amphibious assault ship
	LPH	amphibious assault ship (landing platform helicopter)
M	**MINURSO**	United Nations Mission for the Referendum in Western Sahara
	MMCA	Military Maritime Consultative Agreement
	MND	Ministry of National Defense
	MOOTW	military operations other than war
	MPS	Ministry of Public Security
N	**NATO**	North Atlantic Treaty Organization
	NBC	nuclear, biological, chemical
	NEO	noncombatant evacuation operation
	NGO	nongovernmental organization

	NSG	National Security Guard [India]
	NTS	nontraditional security
P	**PAP**	People's Armed Police
	PKO	peacekeeping operations
	PLA	People's Liberation Army
	PLAN	PLA Navy
	PRC	People's Rebulic of China
R	**R2P**	responsibility to protect
	RECAMP	Reinforcement of African Peacekeeping Capabilities
S	**SAREX**	search-and-rescue exercise
	SARS	severe acute respiratory syndrome
	SCO	Shanghai Cooperation Organization
	SDRA	Swedish Defence Research Agency
	SHADE	Shared Awareness and Deconfliction
	SLOC	sea line of communications
U	**UN**	United Nations
	UNAMET	UN Mission in East Timor
	UNAMID	African Union/UN Hybrid Operation in Darfur
	UNCLOS	UN Convention on the Law of the Sea
	UNPKO	UN peacekeeping operation
	UNSC	UN Security Council
	UNTAET	UN Transitional Administration in East Timor
	USCG	U.S. Coast Guard
	USNORTHCOM	U.S. Northern Command
W	**WMD**	weapons of mass destruction
	WTO	World Trade Organization

About the Contributors

Dennis BLASKO, Lieutenant Colonel, U.S. Army (Ret.), served twenty-three years as a military intelligence officer and Foreign Area Officer specializing in China. Mr. Blasko was an army attaché in Beijing and in Hong Kong from 1992 to 1996 and is the author of *The Chinese Army Today: Tradition and Transformation for the 21st Century,* second edition (Routledge, 2012).

Bates GILL was appointed as director of the Stockholm International Peace Research Institute (SIPRI) in 2007. Prior to this position, he led China-focused programs at the Center for Strategic and International Studies, the Brookings Institution, and the Monterey Institute.

Lyle GOLDSTEIN is associate professor in the China Maritime Studies Institute at the U.S. Naval War College and also visiting fellow at the Watson Institute for International Studies at Brown University. He served as the founding director of CMSI during 2006–2011.

Kristen GUNNESS is senior international policy analyst at the RAND Corporation. Previously, she served as the director of the Navy's Asia Pacific Advisory Group, where she advised the Chief of Naval Operations on China security and maritime issues.

GUO Peiqing is professor at the School of Law and Politics, Ocean University of China.

PAN Zhenqiang, Major General, PLA (Ret.), is currently senior adviser to the Council of China Reform Forum. Major General Pan served in the Department of the General Staff for over two decades and then subsequently as director of the Institute of Strategic Studies at China National Defense University.

PANG Zhongying is professor of international relations and the founding director of the Center for the Study of Global Governance at Renmin University of China in

Beijing. He was a visiting fellow at the Brookings Institution in Washington, D.C., from 2007 to 2008.

Andrew SCOBELL is senior political scientist at the RAND Corporation. He is author of *China's Use of Military Force: Beyond the Great Wall and the Long March* (Cambridge University Press, 2003), and coauthor of *China's Search for Security* (Columbia University Press, 2012).

Gregory STEVENSON received a master of international affairs degree from the Bush School of Government & Public Service at Texas A&M University in May 2010, and completed his bachelor's degree in international relations and Chinese language at Colgate University in 2004.

SUN Kai is assistant professor at the School of Law and Politics, Ocean University of China.

Kathleen WALSH is associate professor of national security affairs. She teaches policy analysis in the National Security Affairs Department of the U.S. Naval War College and is an affiliate of the China Maritime Studies Institute.

XIAO He is a PhD candidate in the School of International Studies, Peking University and Waseda University joint program.

YOU Ji is associate professor in the School of Social Science at the University of New South Wales in Australia. He has written three books and published widely on China's political, military, and foreign policies.

YU Wanli, PhD, is associate professor in the School of International Studies, Peking University, deputy director of the Institute for China-U.S. People-to-People Exchanges, and the academic committee member of the Center for International Studies.